DR. DANNY FORSHEE

"Jesus never challenged His followers to do what He was not already doing. Jesus is a soul winner; Jesus was a soul winner. "For The One" will instruct, encourage, and inspire you in personal witnessing with joy."

DR. JOHNNY HUNT, NORTH AMERICAN MISSION BOARD
SENIOR VICE PRESIDENT OF EVANGELISM AND LEADERSHIP

"Danny Forshee is real. He really loves Jesus, and really loves people who don't know Jesus. That identity comes out in his writing; like the reader is in the company of someone who has a singular love for, and understanding of, evangelism. And, in the spirit of his mentor Roy Fish, it's contagious. Read and be motivated to love people who don't know Jesus!"

STEVEN SMITH, PASTOR
IMMANUEL BAPTIST CHURCH, LITTLE ROCK, AR

"An evangelist tells people how to know God. Thus, Jesus is the greatest evangelist ever. He is the exclusive "way, truth and life"– the only mediator between God and men. In For the One, Dr. Danny Forshee masterfully explains how Jesus led people one-by-one to be forgiven of sin and to know God personally. This is a masterful work about the Master Evangelist. I highly recommend it."

STEVE GAINES, PhD
PASTOR, BELLEVUE BAPTIST CHURCH, MEMPHIS, TN
FORMER PRESIDENT OF THE SOUTHERN BAPTIST CONVENTION

"I consider Danny Forshee a friend, a fellow pastor and a passionate follower of Jesus Christ. Danny's book, "For The One" is an incredible reminder of the heart of God for his lost children. Till every soul around us has knelt at the cross of Jesus Christ, we can never rest. Thank you Danny for reminding us all of our great calling."

RANDY PHILLIPS, LEAD PASTOR, LifeAustin
FOUNDER, PHILLIPS CRAIG AND DEAN

"Jesus saw, valued, and connected with each one of the individuals He engaged while He walked among us. In For the One, Danny Forshee captures these moments in fresh, revealing pictures, showing us how to meaningfully love and lead people to God. Immerse yourself into these snapshots of love and come away with the heart of Jesus."

TIM HAWKS, LEAD PASTOR
HILL COUNTRY BIBLE CHURCH, AUSTIN, TEXAS

"If a deeper devotion to Jesus and longing desire to be equipped to share His love are your heart's passion, then this book by my friend, Dr. Danny Forshee is for you! Christ is our Cornerstone who gives stability and structure to all of our lives as His disciples. Dr. Forshee's study fixes our eyes on Jesus, moving us to share the contagious hope within us to people in our daily traffic patterns of life."

DR. MICHAEL LEWIS, LEAD PASTOR
ROSWELL STREET BAPTIST CHURCH, MARIETTA, GEORGIA

"Ministry is the combination of spiritual depth and people skills. It's taking amazing Biblical truth and connecting with real people in a way that makes an impact. Of course there's no better person to learn this from than Jesus Christ. His life is the epitome of heavenly truth connecting with earthly life. Dr. Forshee gives us application and inspiration from the life of Jesus so that we can make an impact in the lives of those we love as well. Allow "For the One" to set your heart on the road of impact!"

GREGG MATTE
PASTOR OF HOUSTON'S FIRST BAPTIST CHURCH
AUTHOR OF "DIFFERENCE MAKERS"

Title: For The One

Author: Dr. Danny Forshee

Copyright © 2019 Dr. Danny Forshee.

ISBN: 978-0-9988115-9-8

Unless otherwise indicated, all Scripture quotations are taken from Christian Standard Version of the Bible. (2009); Nashville: Holman Bible Publishers.

Published by: Engedi Publishing LLC, in the United States of America

SIGN UP FOR

DANNY'S DAILY DEVOTIONAL

Follow this link to Danny's webpage and fill out your contact information to receive a daily devotional via email. Signup is at bottom of homepage.

www.dfea.com

Or move your smartphone camera over this QR code to go directly to the page.

FOREWORD

I have taught through the years that Jesus never made any demand of us that He had not already embraced in His own personal life. Jesus Himself is the soul winner. Time and time again He personalized this ministry in His life, as you will see in Dr. Danny Forshee's book, For the One. Jesus led men and women one-on-one to a personal relationship with Himself. I am grateful that He did what every pastor must do; He modeled for us pastors what we must do for our people. As we model the message of the gospel of Jesus, we will see others come to Him, just as Jesus saw the fruit of His own ministry.

I pray you will read this book and pass it on. May God begin a movement as you think of the One that God has laid on your heart, given you a relationship with, and who can come to Christ because of the power of the gospel and your intentionality of making Him known to your family, your friends, your work associates and your neighbors.

May God give a great harvest.

Blessings,

Johnny Hunt
Senior Vice President of Evangelism/Leadership,
North American Mission Board
Former Pastor, First Baptist Church Woodstock, GA
Former President Southern Baptist Convention

DEDICATION

To our children Hannah, Bryant, and Leighton—blessings from God and co-laborers for the Gospel.

TABLE OF CONTENTS

INTRODUCTION

This book is based on the life of Jesus Christ and how He fulfilled His mission here on earth, the plan the Father laid out for Him. God the Father had a plan or will for His Son and Jesus obediently fulfilled and obeyed that plan.

We are going to investigate the life of Jesus Christ and the way He dealt with people with whom He came in contact.

One of my favorite hobbies is to read biographies and autobiographies. I recently read two very divergent biographies, one on the reformer Martin Luther and the other on the third president of the United States, Thomas Jefferson. As I read the accounts of their lives, I gained an understanding of the time period in which they lived.

There are four biographies of Jesus and we know them well as Matthew, Mark, Luke, and John. To some readers they are interesting stories, revealing the life of Jesus, who some believe to be a mythical figure, a social reformer, a moral teacher. Those who believe the Gospels and what they actually say about Jesus, however, wholeheartedly believe that Jesus Christ is the Son of God.

Around the same time that I began to study Jesus and His love for the one, a friend gave me a copy of the December 2017 National Geographic journal. The cover of the magazine reads, "The Real Jesus: What Archaeology Reveals about His Life." My first thought was, "This will not be good," but I was pleasantly surprised and so much so that I wrote the author of the article a note of thanks. It is wonderful to see how archaeology continues to confirm the veracity of Scripture.

What a blessing it is to study the real Jesus, the one revealed to us in the Gospels. As we study the encounters He had with men and women in the Bible, we learn not only more about our Savior but also more about how we can love the one and share how they can know Jesus and be blessed.

One of the men who deeply impacted my life was the late Dr. Roy Fish, esteemed professor at Southwestern Baptist Theological Seminary. I give him credit for his contribution to this study, as he gave me his lecture notes entitled, "Evangelism in the Ministry of Jesus." The places where I have quoted him in this book are from those notes.

My prayer is that God would speak powerfully to you through the life of Jesus. The chief objective in writing this book is for you to know Jesus better and share Him more effectively. As you read and also study the sacred Scriptures that describe for us the life of Christ, may you worship God in spirit and in truth. You cannot help but grow spiritually strong as you feast upon the nutrients of God's awesome Word. As a result, you will be emboldened to go and tell others about Jesus— both who He is and how He has changed your life.

You and I cannot help but be changed as we study the way Jesus won others to Himself. By analyzing His life we will become more sensitive to people, better equipped to minister, serve and share Christ with them, and we will simply become better people as we study the greatest person who ever lived.

Everyone we meet needs hope. As followers of Christ, we know the Source of hope. What a joy, privilege, and yes, a responsibility for us to share that hope. "When Jesus is on our minds," as Dr. Chuck Kelley of New Orleans Baptist Theological

Seminary, so memorably put it, "He comes out of our mouths." That is so true.

Ashley and I were at Starbucks recently. She got off work and asked to take me to coffee. Now that sounded good to me. We sat there and were talking about how important it is that we as a church tell people and show people how great God is. A couple was sitting within a few feet of us. We complimented them on their obedient dog sitting quietly beside them. I then said, "Hey, we would like for you guys to come to our church." They threw their coffee in the trash, got very angry, and stormed out of Starbucks. Not! Just the opposite! They said, "We are new to Austin and looking for a church home." They told me five times, "We are out this weekend but will be there after that."

The goal of this book is to learn with the goal of application. Learning without application leads simply to scholarship. I do not want us to be straight as a gun barrel and just as empty! Application without learning leads to superficial Christianity. We need both learning and application as we seek to be holistic and complete in our relationship with Christ.

The motto at Southeastern Baptist Theological Seminary in Wake Forest, NC is "scholars on fire." I love this, not only for seminary students but also for local churches. My desire for you is that you will be disciples making disciples, that you will have deep roots in the faith and be able to live the life and share Christ with others. Seldom if ever will a Christian share his or her faith if they are not abiding in Christ.

There are numerous accounts in Scripture of Jesus dealing with people on a personal level. Jesus clearly stated His purpose for coming to earth in Luke 19:10, "For the Son of Man has come to seek and to save that which was lost."

Okay, buckle up and prepare to be inspired and challenged by the greatest soul winner ever—Jesus Christ!

CHAPTER 1

JESUS

"What man among you, who has one hundred sheep and loses one of them, does not leave the ninety-nine in the open field and go after the lost one until he finds it?"

—LUKE 15:4

In this chapter, we will closely examine how Jesus was prepared and equipped to witness.

JESUS PURSUED THE ONE

1. JESUS CLEARLY UNDERSTOOD HIS MISSION.

Jesus knew He was a missionary. I heard someone say one time, "God had only one Son, and He made Him a missionary."

In order for us to lead others to Christ, we must know the Lord and understand our mission on earth. Our mission is the same as His—to seek and save the lost, to pursue that one lost soul.

Just as we live a life of worship 24/7, we also are to be aware that we are to point people to Christ 24/7 by what we say and how we live.

One of the things I say when beginning a witness encounter is, "You know, I love the Lord and I love people and my job here on earth is to connect the two."

Another way I begin spiritual conversations is, "God is for you; He is not against you."

I do not believe we have any chance encounters as followers of Christ. God brings people into our paths every day in work, study, and play, wherever we are, in order that we might point them to Christ.

When you understand your mission is to love people and point them to Christ, you seize those moments when God brings someone in your path.

Chris Cruz is a good friend of mine who lives in Virginia. I was his pastor years ago. Chris is brilliant; he was a NASA engineer for seventeen years before starting his own company in financial planning and God has greatly blessed him. He is one of the most generous and blessed people I know.

While on a mission trip to New Mexico he was told by the team leader, "You will not be witnessing to people, but just helping out in other ways."

But God had other plans! While Chris was driving the church van by himself, he noticed this big burly guy was following him on a motorcycle. Wherever Chris went, the guy followed him.

Chris became a little concerned and pulled over and motioned for the guy to go around him, but instead the motorcycle pulled up next to Chris. There was a lady sitting behind the man. He asked Chris if he was a part of that group from the church, and Chris said yes. Then he asked if Chris was a preacher. Chris said no, and the guy said, "Good, because I do not trust them!"

Next, the guy asked Chris, "Do you believe what is written on the van?" referring to a Christian statement. Chris said, "Yes, I do."

At this point, the man opened up and said, "For the last few years, I have been searching for something in my life that I am missing. Can you tell me what I need to do?"

Chris shared the story of Jesus with him, and the plan of salvation. The man said, "That is what I need."

Chris then said, "Well, I guess I can pray with you and you can pray." That's what they did, and the man gave his life to Christ! The lady on the bike never said anything; she just sat and listened.

2. JESUS WAS DEDICATED TO ACCOMPLISHING THE FATHER'S WILL.

"Jesus replied, 'Truly I tell you, the Son is not able to do anything on his own, but only what he sees the Father doing. For whatever the Father does, the Son likewise does these things'" (John 5:19).

Would it not be awesome if we could have such an intimacy with Jesus Christ that whatever we see Him doing in Scripture that is what we do?

What amazes me as I read the Gospel of John is the relationship between the Father and the Son. Jesus walked in closeness and intimacy with the Father, and He completely gave Himself to accomplishing the Father's will both in life and in death.

We see this most clearly in Philippians 2:5-11, known as the *kenosis* passage. Philippians 2:7-8 says, "Instead He emptied Himself by assuming the form of a slave, taking on the likeness of men. And when He had come as a man in His external form, He humbled Himself by becoming obedient to the point of death—event to death on a cross."

Jesus made Himself of no reputation. *Kenosis* is the Greek verb meaning to empty; He emptied Himself of divine privileges but not divine essence. I preached on this text while I was at the Yokota Air Force Base outside Tokyo, Japan in August 2006. Lieutenant General Bruce Wright had invited me to come and lead a chaplain's conference. We had quite a diverse group in that military conference room; we had a Catholic priest, Lutherans, one Mormon chaplain, a Southern Baptist, and others.

I preached Christ and this great passage of Scripture. You might argue with me and say about yourself, "This is a little deep for me, a layman; I understand you challenging seminary students and chaplains, but I am just a layman."

I could not disagree with you more! I am raising the bar of expectation for you. With God's help, I desire to encourage you to share Jesus with the one, or as my friend Terry Hurt says— "For the one, in honor of the One, being Jesus Christ!"

3. THE HOLY SPIRIT FILLED OR ENDUED JESUS WITH POWER.

"When Jesus was baptized, he went up immediately from the water. The heavens suddenly opened for him, and he saw the Spirit of God descending like a dove and coming down on him" (Matthew 3:16).

"Then Jesus was led up by the Spirit into the wilderness to be tempted by the devil" (Matthew 4:1).

The Spirit led Jesus to a difficult task. How many of us are being led by God to accomplish difficult tasks? If we are not, then are we filled with the Spirit of God? Just food for thought for you!

4. JESUS WAS COMPASSIONATE TOWARD PEOPLE.

"Jesus continued going around to all the towns and villages, teaching in their synagogues, preaching the good news of the kingdom, and healing every disease and every sickness. When he saw the crowds, he felt compassion for them, because they were distressed and dejected, like sheep without a shepherd. Then he said to his disciples, 'The harvest is abundant, but the workers are few. Therefore, pray to the Lord of the harvest to send out workers into his harvest'" (Matthew 9:35-38).

Jesus genuinely cared for people. This is most conspicuous when you read His dealings with the people He encountered in the New Testament. You have heard this saying or adage before but it is worth repeating—"People do not care how much we know until they know how much we care." It is all about people. The person who says he loves Jesus but cannot stand people does not really love or even know Jesus.

When I was visiting with Lt. General Wright in Japan, I watched how he cared for his military personnel, even opening the door for them! I mentioned to him that I appreciated the way he spoke to the people and stopped what he was doing and acknowledged them; and he told me something simple and yet very profound—"I love these people."

I encourage you who are leaders, whether in the church or in the business world, tell those you serve that you love them and how honored you feel to be their pastor, supervisor or leader.

Jesus showed kindness and compassion through words, tears, and deeds:

a. His words of compassion to the adulterous woman: "Neither do I condemn you; go and sin no more" (John 8:11).

b. His tears of compassion in John 11:35, "Jesus wept." Jesus wept over the death of Lazarus as He witnessed firsthand the sorrow of His people in the face of death.

c. His deeds of compassion in Matthew 9:36-38. The Greek word translated compassion is *esplagna*, and it means to be moved viscerally, emotionally to the point of action.

Pray and ask God that you would be a hearer of the word and a doer. Ask Him to put someone in your path that you can serve and share with this week. But please be careful what you ask for because you just might get it!

This is a prayer God always seems to answer in my life—"Help me share You with someone today."

"Lord, lay some soul upon my heart,
And love that soul through me;
And may I bravely do my part to win that soul for Thee.
Some soul for Thee, some soul for Thee,
This is my earnest plea;
Help me each day, on life's highway,
To win some soul for Thee."[1]

Recently I heard the testimony of Nasser, a man from Saudi Arabia who lives in the USA and was a Muslim Jihadist. Through prayer and through people who lovingly shared the truth of Jesus with him, and also through supernatural dreams that he had, he came to faith in Christ.

Nasser said that happened over 20 years ago. He is now in the ministry and reaching out to those who like him are from a Muslim background. He told us the story of a Muslim man in Wichita, Kansas, who was befriended by a Christian family and invited to Thanksgiving lunch. The man had no idea what Thanksgiving was. The family lovingly embraced him and shared Jesus with him.

This really made him think about Jesus. He called out to Jesus and said, "Jesus, if you are who You say You are, then let me meet someone from my country who can relate to me."

The next day while at a party, he met Nasser. Not only were they from the same country they were from the same city. Their dads lived just a few streets apart.

This Muslim man had a dream about the father in the family that had been so gracious to him at Thanksgiving. The father's name was Don. In the dream, Don was standing on a mountain with snow around him, with a huge smile on his face and with such peace.

The next day the family called this man and said that while on their ski vacation, the father of their family, Don, was in a fatal accident and was killed.

Muslims believe in the power of dreams. They believe that if you have a dream about a person that you respect, that is powerful. Even though Don was a Christian, this Muslim man respected him. In this dream he knew that Don was in heaven. This Muslim man gave his life to Christ.

God loves people and He pursues them for salvation. In His sovereign plan, however, He has chosen to include Christians in the process. Unfortunately, I believe there are many more people interested in Jesus than there are those of us willing to share Jesus. It is about the one. God loves the one lost soul. He will lead us to people who need Him if we will be open.

5. THOUGH SINLESS, JESUS LOVED SINNERS.

Jesus was sinless, yet He associated with people. "He made the one who did not know sin to be sin for us, so that in him we might become the righteousness of God" (2 Corinthians 5:21).

"When the scribes who were Pharisees saw that he was eating with sinners and tax collectors, they asked his disciples, 'Why does he eat with tax collectors and sinners?' When Jesus heard this, he told them, 'It is not those who are well who need a doctor, but those who are sick. I didn't come to call the righteous, but sinners'" (Mark 2:16-17).

Jesus was perfect and never sinned, and yet He loved to be with sinners. People did not bother or intimidate Him. He hung around them.

As we seek to reach people in our cities and towns, it will take more than a come and see mentality or approach. It will take a more incarnational approach where we associate with people, hang out with them and are the hands and feet of Jesus. John Maxwell has said on numerous occasions, "Everything rises and falls on leadership." I would like to submit for your consideration this statement: "Everything rises and falls on relationships."

We share Christ out of our relationship with Christ. If there is sin in our lives and we are not walking with God, rest assured you and I will not talk about Jesus. It is a spiritual endeavor to go and tell. You and I must be filled with the Holy Spirit, and humbly walking with God in order to witness. I believe herein lies the primary reason we do not share. I don't think it is so much a fear of failure or fear of rejection as it is a lack of following Jesus. If we are following Him, we will share Him.

Begin today with a prayer of commitment to the Lord that you desire to be pure and filled with the Spirit so that you will recognize the opportunities God gives you and also take advantage of those opportunities to share Him with others.

6. Jesus was a person of prayer.

"After dismissing the crowds, he went up on the mountain by himself to pray. Well into the night, he was there alone."

—MATTHEW 14:23

"Very early in the morning, while it was still dark, he got up, went out, and made his way to a deserted place; and there he was praying."

—MARK 1:35

If the greatest person to ever live felt it necessary to spend extended time with the Father in prayer, what does that say to you and me?

I have often said that no one preaches any better than he prays. However, the same is true for our witness—none of us witness any better than we pray. Remember—If Jesus is on our mind He will come out of our mouths.

7. JESUS KNEW THE SCRIPTURES.

In the temptation narrative in Matthew 4, we see Jesus quoting from the Old Testament. On three occasions He said, "It is written" and then quoted from the Book of Deuteronomy. He gives us a perfect example to follow. We cannot quote that which we do not read and memorize!

Dr. Roy Fish said Jesus referenced the Old Testament 160 times, referring to two-thirds of the books of the Old Testament.

I encourage you to spend time with God in the Scriptures every single day. First thing in the morning, before TV, or social media, spend that time with God in Bible reading and prayer and watch what a difference God will make in your life!

8. JESUS ASKED MANY QUESTIONS!

I highly recommend to you Randy Newman's book, *Questioning Evangelism*. This is an excellent book written on the discipline of evangelism. The premise of this book is that, as you share Christ with people, ask more questions.

Be more Socratic and dialogical and less declarative. Of course there is a time to declare, but we should also listen more and dialogue when conversing with people.

Ask questions such as: How long have you believed that? Have you considered what the Bible says about this? Newman writes, "If Jesus teaches us anything about evangelism, it's that He used a variety of methods with a variety of people."[2]

JESUS DEALT WITH ALL KINDS OF PEOPLE

1. JESUS MINISTERED TO ALL CLASSES OF PEOPLE.

Jesus dealt with the rich and the poor, religious and irreligious, the outcasts, the lepers, the hurting, the down and out and the up and out. Someone said that we as Southern Baptists do a much better job ministering to the down and out than to the up and out.

I will tell you that the up and out need the Lord as well. Whether it is the rich young ruler or the woman with an issue of blood who spent all her money on her illness, Jesus shared with them, and we too must share with all no matter their socio-economic status.

2. MAN-MADE BARRIERS DID NOT HINDER JESUS.

Jesus touched people from different backgrounds as far as race, religion, and gender.

3. JESUS SPENT MUCH TIME WITH THE SPIRITUALLY NEEDY.

Also called the poor in spirit, they were more receptive to Him and His ministry. He was called a friend of what? Sinners.

"The Son of Man came eating and drinking, and they said, 'Look, a glutton and a drunkard, a friend of tax collectors and sinners!' Yet wisdom is vindicated by her deeds."

—MATTHEW 11:19

JESUS USED SCRIPTURE DEALING WITH PEOPLE

1. JESUS QUOTED THE WORD OF GOD WITH REVERENCE AND RESPECT.

In Matthew 4:4,7,10, Jesus prefaced the quotation from the Old Testament with these words, "It is written."

2. JESUS REGARDED SCRIPTURE AS AUTHORITATIVE WHEN PROPERLY INTERPRETED.

Some, such as Satan and the Pharisees, would misuse the Scriptures for their selfish gain.

"Then the devil took him to the holy city, had him stand on the pinnacle of the temple, and said to him, 'If you are the Son of God, throw yourself down. For it is written: 'He will give his angels orders concerning you, and they will support you with their hands so that you will not strike your foot against a stone.'"

—MATTHEW 4:5-6

"You pore over the Scriptures because you think you have eternal life in them, and yet they testify about me. But you are not willing to come to me so that you may have life."

—JOHN 5:39-40

3. JESUS USED SCRIPTURE FREQUENTLY AS HE DEALT WITH MEN AND WOMEN.

"Just as Moses lifted up the snake in the wilderness, so the Son of Man must be lifted up."

—JOHN 3:14

To have favor with God and influence on others, you and I must saturate our minds with the Word of God. When God's Word is on our minds it will inevitably come out of our mouths and be reflected in the very way we live our lives.

Charles Haddon Spurgeon was arguably the greatest preacher ever in the history of Christendom. He was a Baptist pastor who served 30 years at the Metropolitan Tabernacle in London, England from 1861 to 1891. Six thousand people would come and hear him preach the Word of God. Listen to his words of advice regarding the high importance we must place on filling our minds with Scripture:

"So it is blessed to eat into the very heart of the Bible until, at last, you come to talk in scriptural language and your spirit is flavoured with the words of the Lord, so that your blood is Bibline and the very essence of the Bible flows from you."[3]

JESUS DEALT WITH SIN IN THE LIVES OF PEOPLE

1. JESUS WAS COMPASSIONATE AND YET DIRECT.

We see in John 4:13-14 that Jesus was compassionate as He spoke of living water with the woman at the well and in John 4:16-18 that he was direct as He told her to go call her husband. Jesus knew she had been married to five husbands and that the one she was living with was not her husband!

John 8:11 is also a great example of both compassion and directness in one verse! "'Neither do I condemn you,' said Jesus. 'Go, and from now on do not sin anymore.'"

One of our church members told me about a conversation he had recently with a man who was having a hard time with his job. Our church member was compassionate toward the person and listened to him, but then he told him something very true and also very direct. He said, "Since I turned my business over to the Lord and started tithing, things have been wonderful."

2. JESUS LOVED THE SINNER BUT NOT THE SIN.

This is evident as we look at Zacchaeus' life and how Jesus talked to him in Luke 19:1-10.

3. JESUS WAS TACTFUL.

Here are two examples of His direct, yet tactful, speech with Nicodemus:

"Jesus replied, 'Truly I tell you, unless someone is born again, he cannot see the kingdom of God.'"

—JOHN 3:3

"'Are you a teacher of Israel and don't know these things?' Jesus replied."

—JOHN 3:10

4. JESUS SPOKE OF THE HIGH DEMANDS OF DISCIPLESHIP EVEN IF IT MEANT SOME WOULD BE OFFENDED AND TURN AWAY.

Consider how Jesus spoke to the rich young ruler in Mark 10:21-22, and how He spoke to the crowds in John 6:65-66.

You have heard the expression "To know him is to love him." That is so true when it comes to Jesus Christ—to know Him is truly to love Him. There would certainly be more Christians in the world if there were more Christians! What I mean by this is if we really knew the Jesus of the Bible and lived like He lived, people would be drawn to Him. Sadly, many are only seeing a misrepresentation of Jesus and they are turned off. Two notable examples of this are Mahatma Gandhi and John Lennon as both expressed interest in Jesus Christ but were discouraged to follow Him because of the lives of some of His followers.

I challenge you and encourage you to open your hearts and minds to who Jesus really is, and learn about Him, understand who He is. When you do this, you will begin to respond the way He responded, say what He would say, care like He cared, pray like He prayed, do what He would do, and yes, be blessed and joyful as He was blessed and joyful.

It is entirely possible that, as you are reading this book about Jesus, you realize that you do not know Him; you know about Him but do not have a personal relationship with Him. You may discern that your attitude and actions are so alien and foreign to His. Go to Jesus today in repentance and faith and be saved.

FOR
THE
ONE

CHAPTER 2

JOHN THE BAPTIST

"He must increase, but I must decrease."

—JOHN 3:30

I watched in tears the documentary FOX did on Billy Graham: *An Extraordinary Journey*. It was excellent and it was so true to who Billy Graham was. He was all about Jesus and the Gospel. He would preach or go on these talk shows and focus on Christ and the cross. Like John the Baptist, Billy Graham was all about Jesus increasing and himself decreasing (John 3:30). That is what made Graham the great man and evangelist that he was.

John the Baptizer was such a fascinating man, the cousin of our Lord, and a passionate prophet. John was very religious. But his religion was different than the Pharisees of the day. John was for real. He did not use religion as a means to a greater end. His greater end was God. In fact, he rebuked the religious elite of his day forcefully, as did Jesus. In Matthew 3:7, John called these men a brood of vipers.

Studying the Bible and having knowledge is very praiseworthy. However, my objective is not simply to teach and to fill minds with knowledge. We have to be careful at this point. What happened to the Pharisees also happens to many today in the church—knowledge, as Paul says in 1 Corinthians 8:1, puffs up. We become very knowledgeable and yet do not put into practice the biblical knowledge we possess. When this happens, we become judgmental and mean. The greatest way to combat this tendency is to put into practice the knowledge you possess—love God and love people.

I so enjoyed a recent email from one of our church members as he is living out his life for the one. Tom Ogunleye has a PhD in medical physics. But far from being puffed up with knowledge, Tom is a passionate and humble witness for Christ. As I was leaving for South Asia I got the e-mail all pastors desire to get, especially on a Monday morning! Thank You Lord!

Beloved brother,

Just wanting to let you know we'll be praying for you and the team as you visit our Unengaged, Unreached People Groups. We praise the Lord for what He's doing among them. We also praise the Lord for the message this morning.

O that the Holy Spirit would stir us to never neglect "the one." I travelled out to Corpus Christi for a meeting yesterday. The Lord provided opportunity to witness to three different people and one couple. One of the people—Rebecca—whom I met in front of a Starbucks restaurant, prayed to receive Christ. The couple approached me while I was waiting for my flight in Houston. They started a conversation with me that allowed me to share my testimony with them, give them a Testament and was only able to show them the plan of salvation before we boarded the plane. They are from Leander and I'm reaching out to them.

Thank you again for always holding high the word of God.

See you when you get back.

God bless,

Tom

As we study the life of John the Baptist, we will grasp a better understanding of who he was and the role he played in God's redemptive plan. We will study the one time that Jesus had face to face dealings with John, at Christ's baptism.

THE BIOGRAPHY OF JOHN THE BAPTIST

John the Baptist is one of the truly great and fascinating figures in the history of man. John's life warrants a deeper biographical study:

1. He was our Lord's cousin.

2. He baptized Jesus.

3. John the Baptist has more written about him in the New Testament than anyone except Jesus and Paul.

4. Jesus said of him that none was greater than John the Baptist.

L. R. Scarborough says about John, "John the Baptist was a reformer, a prophet, a mighty preacher, but he was preeminently an evangelist, a soul winning preacher. It is significant that Jesus Christ was introduced to the world by a man whose primary credential was that he was a conquering evangelist and stands out after twenty centuries as one of the most powerful soul-winners the world has ever seen."[4]

Most people that are familiar with John remember his extreme approach to ministry, how he boldly confronted others, how he never cut his hair, how he ate locusts and wild honey, but there is more to the man. Jesus said he was the greatest man born of women.

"Truly I tell you, among those born of women no one greater than John the Baptist has appeared, but the least in the kingdom of heaven is greater than he."

—MATTHEW 11:11

John the Baptist had great character and passion for God. He was willing to live for Christ and to die for Him as well. This is the great need of the hour in our sophisticated 21st century post-Christian world in which we live. We need men and women of radical obedience and passion, who care more about what God thinks of them than what man thinks of them.

John's character was solid as granite; his methods a bit unconventional; and his message straightforward so that no one could misunderstand.

JOHN'S UNIQUE BIRTH

Luke 1:11-17 describes how God chose John for the special calling on his life. John was uniquely set aside by the Holy Spirit to be the forerunner for the Messiah. He was filled with the Holy Spirit while in his mother's womb! His life reminds me of another Old Testament prophet and his unique beginnings.

"I chose you before I formed you in the womb; I set you apart before you were born. I appointed you a prophet to the nations."

—JEREMIAH 1:5

God in His sovereignty sets aside individuals for specific tasks so that He might use them for His glory. Not that I equate my ministry with Jeremiah or John the Baptist, but I will tell you that I knew I would preach before I was saved. I am so grateful that God called me, commissioned me, and set me apart to preach the Word of God.

By the way, your birth was unique as well. No, not in the way John's was, but unique nonetheless. God created you and has a special plan that only you can fulfill. He has uniquely gifted you to serve Him and to build up the body of Christ. Go with your gifting and passion.

Pastor John Piper writes, "Whatever you do, find the God-centered, Christ-exalting, Bible-saturated passion of your life, and find your way to say it and live for it and die for it. And you will make a difference that lasts. You will not waste your life."[5]

JOHN THE PROPHET

"A voice of one crying out: Prepare the way of the LORD in the wilderness; make a straight highway for our God in the desert."

—ISAIAH 40:3

"For he is the one spoken of through the prophet Isaiah, who said: 'A voice of one crying out in the wilderness: Prepare the way for the Lord; make his paths straight!'"

—MATTHEW 3:3

All four Gospel writers contain the Isaiah 40:3 passage. John the Baptist fulfilled this prophecy 700 years after it was written.

John was the last of the Old Testament prophets. As a prophet he preached forceful words, messages that were not easy to hear, but had to be delivered. He blazed the trail for his cousin, Jesus, the Messiah. In Matthew 3:7 John called the religious leaders of the day, the Pharisees and Sadducees, a brood of vipers (den of snakes)!

John was a prophet of God. We still need prophets of God and pastors who preach a prophetic message, whereby we proclaim the truth of God with boldness and love. It is this straightforward, prophetic message that our world must hear. Our world needs prophetic pastors who fear no one but God and would rather offend men than offend God. The message is offensive.

But you cannot preach the true Gospel without offense because you have to tell the truth about sin—we have all sinned and need forgiveness. "For all have sinned and fall short of the glory of God" (Romans 3:23).

Two reasons pastors don't preach like a prophet are that many do not live the message, and some in the congregation do not wish to hear it if he were to preach it.

I read an interesting article from the *Wall Street Journal* entitled "The Perils of 'Wannabe Cool' Christianity" by Brett McCracken. It says that many churches in the USA are compromising their message in an attempt to draw in the twenty-somethings who have left the church in droves. Many churches have sought to be cool, trendy, technologically savvy, and sexy. Some use the topic of sex to try and draw people into church.

McCracken writes, "But are these gimmicks really going to bring young people back to church? Is this what people really come to church for? Maybe sex sermons and indie-rock worship music do help in getting people in the door, and maybe even in winning new converts. But what sort of Christianity are they being converted to?"

McCracken quotes David Wells, who says, "The born-again, marketing church has calculated that unless it makes deep, serious cultural adaptations, it will go out of business, especially with the younger generations. What it has not considered carefully enough is that it may well be putting itself out of business with God."

McCracken concludes his article by writing, "If the evangelical Christian leadership thinks that 'cool Christianity' is a sustainable path forward, they are severely mistaken. As a twenty-something, I can say with confidence that when it comes to church, we don't want cool as much as we want real. If we are interested in Christianity in any sort of serious way, it is not because it's easy or trendy or popular. It's because Jesus himself is appealing, and what he says rings true. It's because the world we inhabit is utterly phony, ephemeral, narcissistic, image-obsessed and sex-drenched—and we want an alternative. It's not because we want more of the same."[6]

John was destined to be a prophet, a preacher, and a preparer for the coming Messiah. He was much less interested in his own life and comfort than he was in fulfilling his mission and mandate.

I encourage you to continue to speak the truth of God in love. Don't back away from the pure gospel. I'm not encouraging you to become Pharisaical and mean-spirited, but to speak the truth. Our job is not to be cool and see how creatively we can convey Christ. Our job is not recreating the gospel message, but simply preaching, continuing, and perpetuating the message we have already received from Christ and His apostles.

If God is calling you to preach, then preach the Word of God as Paul told Timothy: "Preach the word; be ready in season and out of season; rebuke, correct, and encourage with great patience and teaching" (2 Timothy 4:2).

JOHN THE BAPTIZER

The primary activity for which John is known is that he baptized people (Matthew 3:5-6). He even baptized the Lord Jesus Christ (Matthew 3:13-17). *This is the only record where Jesus dealt directly with John.* This momentous event in Jesus' life shows us how important it is for us to follow Christ's example and be baptized.

"Then Jesus came from Galilee to John at the Jordan to be baptized by him. But John tried to stop Him, saying, 'I need to be baptized by You, and yet you come to me?"

Jesus answered him, 'Allow it for now, because this is the way for us to fulfill all righteousness.' Then John allowed him to be baptized.

When Jesus was baptized, he went up immediately from the water. The heavens suddenly opened for Him, and He saw the Spirit of God descending like a dove and coming down on Him.

And a voice came from heaven said, "This is My beloved Son, with whom I am well pleased" (Matthew 3:13-17).

There are two commands, also called ordinances, that the church practices today—baptism and the Lord's Supper. Both Catholics and Protestants believe this to be true, though both groups attach very different meanings or interpretations to these ordinances. Both ordinances are rooted in Scripture, and the Bible clearly commands followers of Jesus to follow through and be baptized and observe the Lord's Supper or Eucharist.

Considering baptism, let's look at these three words: (1) **Humility**, (2) **obedience**, and (3) **blessings**. Only the humble will be baptized, never the proud. Obedience is the key factor when following Jesus' example. God blesses those who follow through in baptism.

1. HUMILITY (MATTHEW 3:13-14)

John was baptizing in the Jordan River; he is called John the Baptist for a reason. Many expressed their turning from sin and embracing God's ways through the waters of baptism.

The mode or method of baptism by John was complete immersion, as the Greek word *baptizo* simply means to submerge. The mode is important because of what it symbolizes. Baptism is a symbol, an outward demonstration that points to an inward change.

Speaking of symbols, when I talk to children about baptism, I use this analogy: I draw a flag on a piece of paper and then put stars and stripes and tell them, "Let's say I put the colors red, white, and blue on the flag. What does this flag represent?" They get it every time; it represents the USA. The colors are not green, orange, and purple, but red, white, and blue. Otherwise, the symbol loses its purpose.

That is how I feel about the mode of baptism; it has to be through full immersion to communicate its primary intent or meaning.

It points to two major themes—one is when we are baptized and go under the water, signifying that our old life has died, a life of sin and selfishness is washed away and we are cleansed from that lifestyle. Now, obviously the H2O or water does not have any cleansing power for the soul, but it does clearly portray the cleansing of the soul by God.

"Or are you unaware that all of us who were baptized into Christ Jesus were baptized into his death? Therefore we were buried with him by baptism into death, in order that, just as Christ was raised from the dead by the glory of the Father, so we too may walk in newness of life."

—ROMANS 6:3-4

The second primary theme is that when one is baptized, he or she is saying with their physical lives, in baptism, "We believe that Jesus Christ is the Son of God who died on the cross and on the third day arose from the dead."

You may ask, "Why wouldn't people want to do this?" Pride, pure and simple. It is a proud heart that keeps people away from following Jesus. Jesus humbled Himself and was baptized as an example for us to follow, not because He had sinned, not because he was in need of forgiveness. At the age of 30 He allowed John to baptize Him.

Humility drips off of this baptism of Jesus like the water that dripped from the clothing of Jesus and John as they stood in the Jordan River.

"But since the Pharisees and experts in the law had not been baptized by him, they rejected the plan of God for themselves."

—LUKE 7:30

It is God's will that you follow Jesus in baptism. Don't be like the proud Pharisees.

My own pride almost kept me from being baptized while a sophomore in college. Like many, I was baptized as a very young child. Some have only been baptized as an infant. I did not understand what I was doing as a young child. No infant can either. For six months I wrestled with the decision, until finally one day I gave up and followed through and was baptized. I am so glad that I did. The burden of conviction was lifted off of my soul once I humbled myself and obeyed God.

2. OBEDIENCE (MATTHEW 3:15)

In Matthew 3:15, we behold both the obedience of Jesus to the Heavenly Father and John's obedience to Jesus.

Jesus obeyed the Father in every way. It was the Father's will for the Son to be baptized. In so doing, Jesus fulfilled all righteousness. He was setting the pattern that true believers would follow. It is a powerful motivation indeed. We call ourselves followers of Jesus, so we should follow His footsteps and His examples.

Next, we see John's obedience. He felt that Jesus should baptize him, but Jesus clearly told him no, I want you to baptize Me. So John did.

I have found in my ministry that those who claim to know Jesus but refuse to be baptized either really don't know Jesus or else they are very ignorant of clear biblical teaching.

"Jesus came near and said to them, 'All authority has been given to me in heaven and on earth. Go, therefore, and make disciples of all nations, baptizing them in the name of the Father and of the Son and of the Holy Spirit, teaching them to observe everything I have commanded you. And remember, I am with you always, to the end of the age.'"

—MATTHEW 28:18-20

Matthew 28:18-20 is a *preaching* or *teaching* of Jesus about baptism. In Acts 8:34-38, looking at Philip and the Ethiopian, we see an *example* of baptism:

"So the eunuch answered Philip and said, 'I ask you, of whom does the prophet say this, of himself or of some other man?' Then Philip opened his mouth, and beginning at this Scripture, preached Jesus to him. Now as they went down the road, they came to some water. And the eunuch said, 'See, here is water. What hinders me from being baptized?'

Then Philip said, 'If you believe with all your heart, you may.'

And he answered and said, 'I believe that Jesus Christ is the Son of God.'

So he commanded the chariot to stand still. And both Philip and the eunuch went down into the water, and he baptized him." (NKJV)

3. BLESSINGS (MATTHEW 3:16-17)

Jesus came up out of the water. You can only come up if you have been down under. Jesus was not sprinkled or poured on; He was dunked, submerged. This mode is the most accurate. It is what Jesus did and the meaning behind the act is so powerful.

Now, please understand that when you get baptized, the heavens will not open and you hear the voice of God. But listen to me carefully, something will happen. God will bless you in ways that only He can. Why? Obedience draws the favor and blessing of God upon your life, just as disobedience and rebellion brings the disfavor and punishment of God upon your life and mine.

It's interesting how at Jesus' baptism in Matthew 3 and also at His Great Commission in Matthew 28, we see the Trinity—the Father, Son, and Holy Spirit.

I try and always tell people that I baptize, "You are going to be blessed."

Changed

I came up out of the water
Raised my hands up to the father
Gave it all to him that day
Felt a new wind kiss my face
Walked away, eyes wide open
Could finally see where I was going
Didn't matter where I'd been
I'm not the same man I was then
I got off track, I made mistakes
Back slid my way into that place
Where souls get lost
Lines get crossed
And the pain won't go away
I hit my knees, now here I stand
There I was, now here I am
Here I am, changed.

—RASCAL FLATTS[7]

JOHN'S LIFE AND MINISTRY

Characteristics of John's life and ministry are revealed to us in God's Word. As we look at these attributes, be sensitive to the Lord speaking to you, in order that these same positive characteristics will be a part of your life as well.

1. JOHN'S PASSION

John was a man full of passion and zeal for our Lord. Even a quick and cursory reading of his life reveals that he was committed, totally sold out to God. His desire was to do God's will for his life. Yes, he was unconventional and a bit unceremonious, but he did what he was called to do. He started where he was; he used what he had, and he did what he could.[8]

John preached, baptized, confronted, trained, and blazed the trail for Christ. You cannot do these things without zeal and passion. Passion is the missing element in many churches and ministers today. I would rather die a passionate death than live one hundred lives of mundane mediocrity, never attempting to do anything great for God.

I have so much respect for Pastor Johnny Hunt. I rejoice in all the good things God has done and is doing at First Baptist Church, Woodstock, in Georgia. While visiting him years ago, I witnessed to a lady at the hotel when I checked in on Wednesday evening and invited her to go to the church. She said, "I have been to that church and that preacher is on fire." I said, "Yes, and if you look up the word passion in the dictionary you would see his picture."

Think how great it would be for people to refer to you or to your church as passionate! How sweet would it be for someone to look up the definition of passionate churches and see a picture of your church!

L. R. Scarborough writes, "This earliest messenger of the gospel planted anew in the deepest souls of redeemed men a burning passion for the salvation of sinful men. It is said of him [John the Baptist] that he was 'a burning and a shining light' (John 5:35). He kindled holy fires around the Master; he brought the divine coal of spiritual passion from the heart of the Master; and thank God, this flaming, kindling fire has spread down through the winding centuries as the mighty creating factor in all evangelistic, missionary, educational and benevolent enterprises today. May that same holy fire burn with renewed glory and power in and from the heart of all those who follow Jesus."[9]

I believe part of John the Baptizer's greatness was his inexorable, relentless commitment to God, his determination to be obedient to God and serve Him no matter what the cost. He was a unique man, the last of the prophets in the line of the Old Testament men who prophesied and foretold of the Messiah's coming. John the Baptist held no punches; he was a powerful man, uniquely equipped and qualified by God to do what he did.

"But when he saw many of the Pharisees and Sadducees coming to his baptism, he said to them, 'Brood of vipers! Who warned you to flee from the coming wrath? Therefore, produce fruit consistent with repentance.'"

MATTHEW 3:7-8

You cannot preach like that without serious passion and fear of God but not man.

HOW PASSIONATE ARE YOU FOR GOD AND THE THINGS OF GOD?

Do you determine what is cool and acceptable and then act, or do you simply serve God out of obedience, not worrying about what people think of you? I read a Beth Moore tweet where she said, "If we have to play dumb to be accepted, make peace with being rejected. Respect others. Walk in humility. But stop playing dumb to make insecure people feel smart."[10]

If there was a passion barometer, a device that could actually measure how bold, zealous, and passionate you are for the LORD, what level would it be on a scale of one to ten, with ten being the greatest? For John, it was all about Jesus and not about John.

2. JOHN'S HUMILITY

John was a humble servant of Christ and I believe this is part of the reason Jesus said that none was greater than John. We have noted his humility in Matthew 3:14 at Jesus' baptism when John said, "I need to be baptized by You, and yet You come to me?"

Here are two more biblical references that point to John's genuine humility: In Mark 1:7, John says he is not worthy to stoop down and untie Jesus' sandal strap. John 1:30 says, "This is the one I told you about: 'After me comes a Man who ranks ahead of me, because He existed before me.'"

John the Baptist was six months older than Jesus (Luke 1:36). However, Jesus was before John, as He was the eternal Son of God. And as we looked at before in John 3:30, John said Jesus must increase "but I must decrease."

What a powerful word for all to say, "May Jesus increase and may I decrease." It is not about what I want and what is in it for me but about God and what He wants. The Bible tells us in Luke 15 what brings heaven great joy, which is lost sinners coming to Him for salvation.

What kind of spiritual unity and revolution would take place in the church today if we all did as John did, dismiss self and exalt Jesus Christ? You see no demanding of rights in John's life; you observe no sense of entitlement where John tells others how important he is and what he deserves; rather, you see one consumed with Christ and his life's mission of preparing the way for Christ and pointing people to the Messiah.

John humbly accepted his position in life as the forerunner, not the main character. His was not the leading man or star in the drama that was real life; rather, he was the supporting and, I might add, subservient character. Scarborough describes John's humility in a memorable way:

"His modesty halted him when Jesus asked to be baptized at his hands. He felt his unworthiness. With the coming of the Master John saw the setting of his own sun. He knew that the night of decrease and defeat and depletion was to gather its solemn curtains around his ministry. He triumphantly announced, 'He must increase; I must decrease.' Oh, what humility, what a glorious surrender! All pride of self, of glory and reputation, all hunger for promotion and position, retired out of the heart of this simple soul-winning preacher as he came face to face with the Master, Jesus, his own Lord."[11]

I urge you to do as Jesus did and take upon yourselves the role of a servant. In Philippians 2:7, Jesus took the *morphen doulou*, the form of a servant, a household slave who did menial tasks. Does that not absolutely astound you? The King of Glory, the Treasure of Heaven Himself came to earth in the form of a slave! May God help us get rid of all pride and truly humble ourselves before the Lord so He can use us to do what He wants us to do!

3. JOHN THE PREACHER

John was indeed a powerful preacher who would not mince words or seek the applause of man. This was due in part because he was a prophet of God. We have already noted his boldness in confronting the religious leaders of his day in Matthew 3:7 by calling them a "brood of vipers." John strongly denounced the religious hypocrites who hated Jesus and orchestrated His death.

John proclaimed Jesus as the Lamb of God who takes away the sin of the world (John 1:29). That was a bold statement. He did not call Jesus "one of the many ways" or "a religious leader who can take away sin"; rather, he said He was the Lamb of God.

Scarborough portrays John's preaching this way—"Kings and governors came to listen and went away to fear. He was great in tenderness; lion-like in boldness; simple, pungent, convincing in speech; powerful like a storm from Lebanon's snowy summits.[12]

In John 3:26-36, John the Baptist gives a response to those who said people are going to Jesus instead of you. John said yes, that is true, and that is great.

I heard Dr. Mark Harris, former pastor of First Baptist Church, Charlotte, North Carolina, preach on this text. Dr. Harris explained it this way:

John the Baptist is like the best man in a wedding, who takes the hand of the groom and the hand of the bride and brings them together. Then the best man simply fades out of the picture.

John preaches a great sermon, recorded in John 3:27-36. Look at how John ends this sermon: "The one who believes in the Son has eternal life, but the one who rejects the Son will not see life; instead, the wrath of God remains on him" (John 3:36).

4. JOHN'S HUMANITY AND DOUBTING

In Luke 7:18-35, John sends some of his disciples to question Jesus, asking if He is the Messiah. John is in prison and he has some doubt regarding Jesus' Messiahship. Morgan writes, "As reports of His [Jesus'] work reached John in prison, it did not seem that He was doing the things that John expected would be done."[13]

Jesus, however, assured John that He was doing what He was supposed to be doing (vs. 22). Then Jesus offers a tender rebuke of John in Luke 7:23. Take a look at what Jesus does in verses 24-28, He builds up John and honors him even though John had just questioned Him!

We also may be tempted to question God's plan and method in our time of doubt and depression, but we must remember that God knows what He is doing. We must trust Him. I am reminded of the powerful quote Johnny Hunt gave me years ago when I was going through a tough time in my ministry, one of doubt and confusion. He said to me, "Do not question in the dark what God revealed in the light."

It is so easy to doubt in the dark. I heard the head basketball coach at the University of Kentucky, Coach John Calipari, tell about their four-game losing streak in 2018 and how his team was discouraged. Coach Calipari told them, "Hang in there, stay with the process, do your part; I have seen it many times before, and you will come through this." And they did come through it; they went on to win the SEC Championship when most had written them off.

5. JOHN'S MARTYRDOM

John's martyrdom is recorded in Matthew 14:3-12. John died because he had a conviction over the sin of Herod and because he used his prophetic voice to confront Herod. He told Herod that sleeping with the wife of his brother, Philip, was wrong. John paid the ultimate price for his convictions.

I read Eric Metaxas' book on Martin Luther; it is a very good read. Luther was most outspoken and passionate for God. At times he was actually disappointed that he did not die a martyr's death.

But many other reformers did die in service to our Lord. One of them was William Tyndale, an English reformer, just as Luther was a German reformer. Today we know Tyndale chiefly for his translation of the Hebrew and Greek biblical texts into the English language. Like John the Baptist, Tyndale spoke out against royalty and called them out in their sin.

"In 1530, he wrote The Practyse of Prelates, opposing Henry VIII's planned annulment of his marriage to Catherine of Aragon in favour of Anne Boleyn, on the grounds that it was unscriptural."[14]

In 1536 he was strangled to death right before his body burned at the stake. Why? He spoke the truth and called people, like Luther did, back to the Bible. He was accused of being a heretic and challenged false beliefs in light of Scripture and it cost him his life. His last words before his death were, "Lord, open the King of England's eyes."[15]

What a tremendous example to us today, especially pastors and ministers in America, where we find ourselves too often concerned over comfort rather than the will of God to suffer. John's love for Jesus and the truth empowered him to preach and live with conviction. It also enabled him to die with conviction. John was not attached to this world. He knew that earth was not his ultimate home. May God help us remember the same truth.

I hope you are encouraged and also challenged by John the Baptist's devotion and commitment to Jesus Christ. I am so glad that his story is recorded in the New Testament, so we can read and be blessed and motivated.

We will conclude with a list of six challenging remarks about John's life from L. R. Scarborough:

1. John had "a deathless passion for the simple truth."

2. He had "a humility that lives at the feet of Jesus."

3. He had "a ministry that rightly introduces and sets forth Jesus the Lamb of God."

4. John was "the kindler of holy fires, the institutor of spiritual passion for the lost."

5. John was a man who consistently would "preach and teach and sing a triumphant gospel in the simplicities of heaven's power."

6. Finally, Scarborough reminds us from the example of John, that we must "be willing to decrease that Christ may increase, be ready to stay, to go, to suffer, to die, to endure, to live, for the introduction of Jesus, the Lamb of God, to a lost world."[16]

John's life was a remarkable one and speaks to all of us wherever we are spiritually. How has God spoken to you through this fiery preacher's life, testimony, ministry, and death?

FOR
THE
ONE

CHAPTER 3

THE PARALYTIC

Seeing their faith, Jesus told the paralytic,
"Son, your sins are forgiven."
But some of the scribes were sitting there,
questioning in their hearts: "Why does he speak like this?
He's blaspheming! Who can forgive sins but God alone?"
Right away Jesus perceived in his spirit
that they were thinking like this within themselves and said to them,
"Why are you thinking these things in your hearts?
Which is easier: to say to the paralytic, 'Your sins are forgiven,'
or to say, 'Get up, take your mat, and walk'?
But so that you may know that the Son of Man has authority
on earth to forgive sins"—he told the paralytic—
"I tell you: get up, take your mat, and go home."
Immediately he got up, took the mat,
and went out in front of everyone.
As a result, they were all astounded and gave glory to God,
saying, "We have never seen anything like this!"

—MARK 12:5-12

God loves to put people in our paths so that we can share Christ with them, serve them, and reach out to them in any way He wants them to be blessed. Jesus gives us a clear pattern or example to follow; there are hurting people everywhere. All that is missing is His church, us, to obey Him.

Recently when I went to the gym to work out. I met a man whom I had never seen before. I had my spiritual antennas up and was ready to find the one and share with him. I just initiated the conversation, started talking to him and invited him to church. He said he works on Sundays at the airport from 6:00am to 2:00pm. He asked about our Wednesday nights and so I invited him to join our men's group called MENtor.

He then began to share with me. He said we all need to be washed in the blood of the Messiah. And he said we are to pray without ceasing. He did not know what that meant as a child but understands now, that all throughout the day we are to keep our minds on God.

We had such good fellowship. Here is the beautiful thing about reaching out to people—you get to share Christ with those who do not know Him, or you find out they are saved, and you get to meet a new brother or sister in the Lord.

There are times when you and I need to initiate the conversation, but then there are times, such as in Mark 2, that the other person begins the encounter. Jeffrey, our student pastor, shared with our staff that a new neighbor knocked on their door and said his family still lives in Beaumont, but he has moved to Austin to work and will move his family eventually. Then he asked Jeffrey, "Do you know any good churches in the area?"

Mark 2:1-12 tells a marvelous story that reveals the power of Jesus Christ not only to heal sick bodies, but also to heal, more importantly, sinful souls. This is the central message of

Christianity—Jesus forgives sins. All other religions are man's attempts to reach God and forgiveness, but Christianity is God reaching down to man to give him what he could never earn, which is a full pardon of sin. This story is also found in Matthew 9:2-8 and Luke 5:17-26.

This man was paralyzed and dependent on the generosity and help of friends, family, and strangers. But even his conspicuous physical need did not overshadow the greater spiritual need that he had. He needed forgiveness of sin that only God can grant.

We need to do all we can to be there for people and help them. I know we cannot help everyone with their physical needs, but we can help every person we meet with their greatest need and that is the forgiveness of sins through Jesus Christ our Lord.

At this time in Jesus' life, His one was this man who needed help in every way. We will look at this amazing miracle of Jesus and study His life and the way He interacted with this paralytic as well as the others in the story. As a result, we will learn how we are to conduct our lives as God allows us to interact with people. There are three truths from this text that I want to highlight. All three are simple—**Preach the Word**, **Bring Your Friends**, and **Watch Jesus Work**.

PREACH THE WORD (MARK 2:1-2)

In Mark 2:1-2, Jesus returns to Capernaum, His Galilean headquarters or base of operation. Capernaum is located in the northern part of Israel on the northern tip of the Sea of Galilee. The home was probably the house of Peter and Andrew (Mark 1:29). In 2008 and 2018, we visited the synagogue and the place where the home of Peter and Andrew was located, as it was located just a few hundred feet from the synagogue. Today it has a church built over the site of the home.

I recall our guide telling us that we will hear often that Jesus was in this area or that area. But there are two places so well documented that we know where He was precisely. One place was this synagogue in Capernaum and the other was the Pool of Bethesda in John 5.

On the second day of our 2008 tour of Israel, we came to the ancient city of Capernaum. It was one of my favorite places. Looking back through my journal, I made these observations about Capernaum:

We then went to Capernaum, one of my favorite places. We saw the home of Peter. Nearby was the very synagogue in which Jesus preached and cast out the unclean spirit that inhabited the man in church that day as recorded in Mark 1:21-28. A Roman centurion who commanded one hundred troops, a Gentile, built the synagogue in Capernaum. Jesus healed his servant (Luke 7).

You never know how far your gifts will go as you give to the Lord and His work. This man built a place of worship that the Lord Himself would visit and preach in! As Bethany was Jesus' primary place where He stayed in Judea (in the home of Mary, Martha, and Lazarus), so Capernaum was His headquarters for His Galilean ministry.

However, this synagogue in Capernaum was destroyed, just as Jesus predicted in Matthew 11:23-24. The city of Capernaum was leveled in AD 66-70 by the Romans and yet again by the devastating earthquake in AD 749. It was never rebuilt. Someone estimated that eighty percent of the miracles of Jesus were performed in Capernaum. This was a neat place for me because it was in this very place and synagogue that Jesus spent time and He preached. It was an impressive building. I remember commenting on how large it was, as I did not envision the synagogues being that large.

In Mark 2:1, word got out that Jesus was in the house. When people heard this, they came. In verse 2, Mark says immediately (*eutheos*)—one of his favorite words—the people came. Even the outside area was congested; there were many people wanting to see and hear Jesus Christ.[17] The house was filled with people because of the presence of God in the house.

People were drawn to Jesus just like people are still drawn to Him when He is present in power. He is no longer present as He was when He walked on earth, but He is still very much present by the powerful presence of the Holy Spirit. When word gets out that God is present in your church, then there will be people who will come and want to meet God.

This is a good word for church growth: How do you grow a church? Well, you do not, that is God's job, but we can work with God by making sure the Lord of His church is welcome and present and not on the outside knocking on the door as He was in Revelation 3:20 at the church of Laodicea.

With a crowd of people gathered together, please make note of what our Lord did; He preached the Word to them. I love it. Jesus was a preacher of the Word of God. The Greek word translated "preach" is *laleo*, which literally means "to speak." (It is in the imperfect active indicative—continuous action in the past.) He was continuing to teach the Word when He was interrupted. When people gather together in the presence of the Lord at church, the pastor must do what Jesus did, which is preach the Word to the people, teach them, and instruct them in the Word of God.

People are hungry to hear the Word of God taught by the man of God in the church of God. It is my highest calling as a pastor. It is the one thing I do consistently that no one else does on our staff and that is okay. This is my passion and as long as God gives me the strength to do it, I want to preach His Word until God takes me home.

A really wonderful way to exit earth and go to the presence of Jesus as a pastor is to do what the great evangelist George Whitefield did. What a mighty preacher of the Word of God. He was a good friend of Benjamin Franklin and an indefatigable preacher, averaging ten sermons a week.

The night before he died, he preached in the open fields for two hours, standing on a barrel in Newburyport, Massachusetts. He was fifty-five years old. In this message, he preached on the futility of trying to be saved by good works. He was a gospel preacher who told his hearers that the only way people can be saved is on the merit of Jesus Christ's death on the cross for their sins.

He said, "Works! works! A man gets to heaven by works! I would as soon think of climbing to the moon on a rope of sand."

Whitefield preached his last message late that evening, holding a candle while standing on the steps outside the place he was staying. The people gathered to hear him preach and so he did, and then went back to bed and died at 6:00am on September 30, 1770.[18]

Remember Paul's command to Timothy?

"I solemnly charge you before God and Christ Jesus, who is going to judge the living and the dead, and because of his appearing and his kingdom: Preach the word; be ready in season and out of season; rebuke, correct, and encourage with great patience and teaching. For the time will come when people will not tolerate sound doctrine, but according to their own desires, will multiply teachers for themselves because they have an itch to hear what they want to hear. They will turn away from hearing the truth and will turn aside to myths."

—2 TIMOTHY 4:1-4

Being ready in season and out of season means when they want to hear the Word or when they do not, or when you feel like preaching it or you do not feel like it. The fact remains that you are to preach the Word of God.

BRING YOUR FRIENDS (MARK 2:3-4)

The paralytic's four faithful friends brought him to Jesus. Walter Wessell describes a typical peasant's home in Israel during this time as a "small, one-room structure with a flat roof. Access to the roof was by means of an outside stairway. The roof itself was usually made of wooden beams with thatch and compacted earth in order to shed the rain. Sometimes tiles were laid between the beams and the thatch and earth placed over them."[19]

The men were concerned for their friend. They were creative in their approach to get this man to Christ. No doubt debris, dirt and dust were falling in the house. I imagine the people in Mark 2:6 were critical. Perhaps Peter and Andrew were thinking, "Wow, there is a hole in my roof!"

However, I see Jesus smiling! These four, faithful friends were passionate and very compassionate; they cared for their hurt friend, and they were so concerned for him that they were willing to tear up a roof to get him in the presence of Jesus Christ.

Here you have a group of four men that I wish every church could have. Not all of us are called to preach publicly, but all of us are called to share with others the Gospel of Jesus and bring our friends in order that they can hear those who are preaching the Word of God. Instead of worrying about getting our needs met, I wish we were engrossed with getting hurting people into God's presence.

What if we were as concerned for souls getting in the presence of Jesus as we are for getting what we want in church? Can you imagine the effort it took to get the man there—they had to go get him and then had to pick him up and carry him up the stairs? It was hard work and took a Herculean effort, but their labors were greatly rewarded by Jesus.

How hard do you labor to get people to church on Sunday to hear your preacher preach the Word of God? True, your preacher is not Jesus, the greatest preacher the world will ever see or hear. But if he is a follower of Jesus, preaching the Word of God so that your friends and lost loved ones can hear and be saved, then are you working to bring others? I have found in my ministry that those in the church who are passionate about the peripheral things in church like the genre and style of music and the clothes they wear are less passionate about bringing souls to Jesus.

WATCH JESUS WORK (MARK 2:5-12)

Mark 2:5 tells us that Jesus saw the faith of all five men in this group, "Seeing their faith, Jesus told the paralytic, 'Son, your sins are forgiven.'"

God is attracted to belief. These five men all had faith that Jesus could heal the sick man. Faith is a beautiful thing. Whereas unbelief closes doors, belief flings open doors to let the power of God come in.

In Matthew 9:2, Jesus tells the paralytic, "Son, be of good cheer; your sins are forgiven you." He addresses him in a tender way and tells him to be of good cheer or to have *tharseo*, courage.

There are a couple of Greek words translated courage; tharseo and *tolmao*; Jesus uses the word *tharseo*, which means a courage that "consists in an absolute absence of fear, which is a far greater thing than the courage, which, in spite of fear, goes forward in activity." [20]

Here is a good interpretation by Eduard Schweizer, of why Jesus healed the man spiritually before He healed him physically: "All suffering is rooted in man's separation from God. For this reason, Jesus must call attention here to man's deepest need; otherwise the testimony of this healing would remain nothing more than the story of a remarkable miracle."[21]

The greatest thing we can do to address systemic, large-scale problems is simply do something; impact the one in your path. This is true for lostness, as most of the world does not know Jesus, and they worship false gods.

We can look at that and respond in one of two ways—first, just do nothing with the thought—there is so much need, what difference can one person make? Or second, have the mindset, true—I can't do everything, and what I do may be small, but I will do something. I will share Jesus with those I meet and seek to help in whatever way God leads me.

Or it is true with racism, or poverty, or injustices like sex trafficking—we can become so overwhelmed and callous to the hugeness of the need that we retreat back into our comfort zones and do nothing. It is a powerful anecdotal story that has been in circulation for years, but I will share it again as it illustrates clearly how all of us can do something and impact the one.

A boy was walking along the seashore and picking up starfish and tossing them in the ocean one by one. An elderly man told the young man it really did not matter what he was doing because there were so many starfish. The boy picked another up, looked at the elderly gentleman, and said, "It matters to this one."

What if all of us had this mindset of "I cannot do everything but I can do something?" I know I cannot reach the entire world but I can reach the person God brings into my world.

I will tell you what will happen—change for the better, lives impacted, our churches exploding in growth and the kingdom of darkness diminished and the kingdom of God expanded.

The greatest example ever of one person changing the world one heart at a time is Jesus Christ. Jesus loved the Father and loved doing the Father's will. It is God's will that none perish but all come to repentance, according to 2 Peter 3:9.

Never doubt what one person can accomplish as long as he or she believes and never gives up. I watched a sports documentary on the Old Ball Coach, Steve Spurrier. What a life he has lived. His dad was a pastor and he learned much from his father. He went on to play baseball, basketball, and football in high school, and then on to the University of Florida to play quarterback and eventually win the Heisman Trophy.

Spurrier began coaching after a short stint in the NFL, and it was in coaching that he found his calling. His first head-coaching job in college was at Duke University. He was successful even at Duke, not known for their football, but for their academics and basketball.

He won the National Championship at Florida and then went on to the NFL to coach the Washington Redskins before becoming a successful coach at the University of South Carolina. Coach Spurrier's great attribute, what makes him so successful, is that he believes, and he inspires others to believe. When he went to Duke, he told them, "We are going to win the ACC Championship" and people thought he was crazy! But he instilled in his players a strong belief and confidence and sure enough, they won the ACC.

Anyone can doubt and not believe, but once you step out of the darkness of doubt and start to believe God for great things, then get ready, because God is attracted to simple, childlike faith.

Jesus forgives sins, reads and rebukes religious minds, and heals the sick.

A. JESUS FORGIVES SINS (MARK 2:5-7)

In verse 5, we see that, as the Son of God, Jesus has the power to forgive and He does so in response to the man's faith in Him.

The scribes or experts in the religious law, mentioned in verse 6, were very powerful people in Israel. Their response was just the opposite of belief; it was unbelief.

They put a question mark where God had placed an exclamation point. Instead of believing in their hearts, they engaged in the analysis of paralysis and concluded that Jesus was a blasphemer.

The religious scribes were judgmental and critical (Mark 2:6-7). The five men who believed would see the favor and blessing of God, but these scribes would receive the rebuke and disfavor of God.

Luke 5:17 points out that the scribes, Pharisees, and teachers of the law had traveled a long way to be there. They had come as far as Jerusalem. No doubt their purpose was to come and criticize or try to catch Jesus in an error.[22]

They did not see what the common people, like the paralytic and his four friends, saw, that Jesus was indeed God in the flesh. They were correct in their theology at least partly, because only God can forgive sins, no one else. But they failed to recognize, as many fail to do today, that in Jesus Christ, the God of the universe has come in human flesh. This is known in the Christian faith as the great doctrine of the Incarnation.

It is the same today—we can respond in faith and trust God and be blessed, or we can question, doubt, criticize, and receive the disfavor of God. The choice is ours to make. The man who believed was forgiven his sins, while the religious leaders remained in their sins.

B. JESUS READS AND REBUKES RELIGIOUS MINDS (MARK 2:8-10)

Jesus read their critical minds and challenged them with a question in Mark 2:9. I like Dr. Wessell's statements here; "Both were alike impossible to men and equally easy for God. To the teachers of the law, it was easier to make the statement about forgiveness because who could verify its fulfillment? But to say, "Get up...and walk"—that could indeed be verified by an actual healing that could be seen."[23]

Mark 2:10 is so important. Jesus tells the scribes, so that they may know (*oida*) in Greek, to know by experience, that the Son of Man has authority (*exousia*).

The title Son of Man was Jesus' favorite self-designation, used 81 times in the New Testament. He is the promised Messiah in the Old Testament who relates to us in our humanity. In Daniel 7, the title Son of Man is used in an exalted way. In John 3:16 and Luke 22:70, He refers to Himself as the Son of God, but by far His favorite title is Son of Man. He loves us, relates to us and has come to save us.[24]

There are three times in Matthew where this word *exousia* is used of Jesus. All three are significant. In Matthew 7:28-29, when Jesus finished preaching the Sermon on the Mount, the people were astonished at His teaching because He taught them with authority, not as the scribes.

In Mark 2, Matthew 9:6, 8, and then again in Matthew 28:18, Jesus says all *exousia* has been given to Him in heaven and on earth. Then He gives the Great Commission to go and make disciples. Morgan writes, "If we take these three outstanding references, we find His ethical authority, His redeeming authority, and His governing authority. At the center therefore is this word of redeeming authority, His authority to say to the troubled soul of man burdened with sin, 'Thy sins are forgiven.'"[25]

C. Jesus heals sick bodies (Mark 2:11-12)

I believe Jesus turns His attention to the paralytic and addresses him with the words in Mark 2:11. Notice the ex-paralytic got up immediately, and he took up his bed as Jesus told him, and then he went out "in full view of them all."[26]

The results were amazement and praise in verse 12. "The significance of this story is not to be understood in terms of Jesus' pity on a helpless cripple that moves Him to heal the man's paralyzed body. The emphasis is on the forgiveness of sins. This was the root of the paralytic's problem, and it was to this that Jesus primarily addressed Himself. In His act of forgiveness Jesus was also declaring the presence of God's kingdom among men."[27]

I agree it was the lesser of the two miracles, but it still amazes me that Jesus healed sick bodies while on the earth. In His sovereign way, He still heals today.

LESSONS TO REMEMBER FROM JESUS' INTERACTION WITH THE PARALYTIC

1. Jesus welcomes hurting people.

We see in this story Jesus' availability to those who hurt. He does not mind the interruption to His preaching. He stops and embraces this man and his four faithful friends.

Hebrews 13:8 says, "Jesus Christ is the same yesterday, today, and forever." He still welcomes those who hurt, and He uses you and me, the church of the living God, to touch and embrace and help those who hurt.

We must learn from Jesus' example, especially those of us called to teach and lead in the church of God. The church is a hospital for sinners, a place of refuge for those battered by the maladies of life and especially the disease of sin.

Another proper analogy of the church is that we are a battle ship and not a cruise ship. I must commend our church at this point—GHBC is a church on mission and does a good job in welcoming and helping the hurting. True, we cannot help everyone, no one church can; but whether it is the Benevolence Ministry, ESL Life Bridge Ministry, or Alzheimer's Respite Ministry, it is a blessing to see our church helping those who hurt, both in our community and around the world.

Are you hurting? You will not bother God, but will find Him most compassionate and receptive to you.

2. JESUS RESPONDS TO FAITH.

Look at what Jesus took special notice of in Mark 2:5. It was not their ingenuity, creativity, or even their determination. Rather, He took note of their faith.

Hebrews 11:1 says, "Now faith is the substance of things hoped for, the evidence of things not seen."

Hebrews 11:6 says, "But without faith it is impossible to please Him, for he who comes to God must believe that He is, and that He is a rewarder of those who diligently seek Him."

These five men had faith and note their faith was in Jesus. The only reason they tore up Peter's roof was because they believed that Jesus could help them.

When Jesus is the object of your faith you will be secure and never disappointed. A group of botanists were in the Alps searching for rare species of flowers when they spotted one at the bottom of a deep ravine. The scientists noticed a small boy standing by and they asked if they could tie a rope around his waist and lower him into the ravine so he could extract the flower.

The little boy looked down into to the deep canyon and told the scientists to wait a minute and he would be back. The boy returned with a man and told the botanists, "I'll go over the cliff now and get the flower for you, but this man must hold on to the rope. He's my dad!"

Just as that earthly father was no doubt pleased with his son's pure trust in him, we can be assured that God is pleased when we put our full trust in Him, and unlike our earthly fathers who can fail, Jesus never fails, but will always respond for our good.

3. JESUS STILL FORGIVES SINS, READS AND REBUKES RELIGIOUS MINDS, AND HEALS BROKEN BODIES.

Jesus basically told the scribes that He will heal the man on the outside so that they would know that He can save the soul on the inside. He wanted them to know that he could do the impossible and that is forgive sins.

When I taught evangelism at Southeastern Baptist Theological Seminary, a missionary doctor by the name of Doug Derbyshire preached in chapel one day. He received his medical degree from the University of Arizona and served in Thailand as a medical missionary.

Dr. Derbyshire preached an excellent sermon on Mark 2, saying that he loves for people to come to him sick and then leave whole. He said that he loves it even more when they are made whole spiritually. This missionary started a study group with some Buddhists and asked them what topic they wished to discuss. They answered unanimously. The topic they wanted to discuss was "How a man can know that his sins are forgiven."

What about you? Has God revealed your need to teach and preach the Word of God, as His Son did so faithfully? Have you been inspired to bring your friends to Christ even as these four men did in our text today?

Are you like the paralytic? You are sick physically and need a miracle from God. You may be whole physically but spiritually your sins have not been forgiven and you need a relationship with Christ. Is the burden of sin and shame wearing you down? God wants to relieve you of your enormous burden of guilt and shame caused by sin. Ask Him to forgive you, to save you, and He will. This man in Mark 2 had faith and Jesus saved him. Have faith in Jesus to save you, and turn from your sins and embrace Jesus as your Savior and Lord.

I know God has challenged me through the efforts of these four men. They were great friends and went the extra mile to get their friend to Jesus. Oh, may we be as committed to bringing our friends to Christ.

CHAPTER 4

ANDREW

As he was walking along the Sea of Galilee,
he saw two brothers, Simon (who is called Peter), and
his brother Andrew.
They were casting a net into the sea—for they were fishermen.
"Follow me," he told them, "and I will make you fish for people."
Immediately they left their nets and followed him.

—MATTHEW 4:18-20

As we study Christ's divine encounter with a man named Andrew, we have another opportunity to study the Master, Jesus Himself. As we study Jesus' life and love for others we are challenged, blessed, and benefited.

Andrew is one of the original twelve disciples of Jesus Christ. He is mentioned eight times in the New Testament. He is the first disciple of Jesus, and he was initially a disciple of John the Baptist.

"He had evidently become conscious of the need for repentance, and had submitted himself to the ritual baptism that indicated the confession of sin, and the desire for remission and renewal."[28]   He was a spiritual man no doubt.

Dr. Fish referred to him as a "religious aspirant." He had aspirations for religious or spiritual things.

There are many like Andrew today, who have a bent or proclivity for spiritual matters and are hungry for real spiritual substance. We should welcome people as Jesus did and spend time with them, helping them understand the Answer to their spiritual thirst.

Andrew was a fisherman by trade. Matthew 4:18-20 tells us he was a fisherman along with his brother Peter. This encounter with Andrew and Peter happened at least a year later than the first encounter in John 1. The name Andrew literally means manly. Like his brother, he was probably a large man, a bold and courageous one as well.

Morgan insightfully writes, "Moreover, he was a man marked by moral courage and insight, as is evidenced by the immediateness of the way in which at a critical moment, he left John [the Baptist], the herald, and followed Jesus."[29]

Look at John 1:35-42. John the Baptist had said the day before, perhaps in Andrew's hearing, "Behold! The Lamb of God who takes away the sin of the world!" John 1:29.

Now he repeats the key statement of Jesus being the Lamb of God in verse 35. That is a significant statement. Jesus was the Lamb from God who would take away the sins of the world through His death and resurrection. No doubt, this intrigued Andrew, who knew about the sacrificial system of lambs slain for the sins of the people.

In John 1:38, Jesus turns to Andrew and John the Beloved and asked them a pointed question, "What do you seek?"

This is a deep question. There is more to it than just a surface inquiry. Jesus is asking them what they are looking for, what they are thinking, why they are coming after Him.

"Jesus was drawing him (Andrew) out by drawing him in."[30]

Notice Andrew's response; he responds with a question. First, he addressed Jesus as Rabbi, or teacher. It is interesting because they have not submitted themselves to His instruction, but they honor Him with this title. They will subsequently come to realize that He is much more than a teacher or Rabbi or prophet; He is none other than the Christ, the Messiah come from God.

Andrew asked Him where He is staying. This answer is more of a request to ponder and think about the question Jesus already posed to him. He is after more than a physical address with his question about where Jesus is staying.

Jesus tells him to come and see. I love that answer. **Jesus wasn't saying come and see where I live, as much as He was saying come and meet with Me and you will find the answer to the spiritual hunger and thirst you have to the deep religious questions you are pondering.**

Andrew and John went with Jesus. We have no record of the time they spent together, but they had an extended time together. John 1:39 says they remained with Jesus that day. The tenth hour could mean that they talked from 10:00 am till sunset. It could also mean that they met at 4:00 p.m., and for the remainder of that day and into the next day.

Tenney says that they stayed with Jesus that day and overnight.[31] Either way, it was a lengthy amount of time and the conversation changed Andrew and John. Perhaps Jesus shared more about John the Baptist's statements in John 1:29 and 36, explaining that He was the Lamb of God who had come to die and save the world. Or perhaps, following up on the word seek and Andrew's disposition to learn more about spiritual things, our Lord shared truths with him related to seeking, such as

Matthew 6:33 or Matthew 7:7-8, or Luke 19:10. [32]

Andrew and John met Christ and they are changed. Notice what Andrew does after his encounter with Jesus. He goes and tells his brother Simon or Peter. He told him they had found the Messiah, the Christ. So much for the difficulty and hesitancy often exhibited when evangelizing our families!

Perhaps Jesus explained to them from the Old Testament that He is the coming One, the Messiah, who has come to save the world from sin and eternal death. Morgan writes, "**Immediately this man became a missionary.**"[33]

Andrew is seen in John 6:8-9, bringing the young boy with the loaves and fish to Jesus, and in John 12:20-22, he is seen bringing the Greeks to Jesus, who requested to see him. Perhaps Andrew thought back to the time when Jesus told him, "Come and see."

Dr. Fish writes, "I don't know anybody in the New Testament who seems to be more interested in bringing people to Jesus than Andrew."

What a privilege, to be known forever in the New Testament as someone who brought others to Jesus Christ, who introduced others to the Messiah, as Andrew did to Peter.

Peter went on to become the great preacher in Acts 2. You never know what will happen and how God will use those whom we have the privilege of introducing to Jesus Christ. Edward Kimball was a Sunday school teacher in Boston in the 1850s and he witnessed to a young shoe clerk. The teen had not finished the fourth grade. This young man accepted Christ as his Savior and Lord and went on to lead a million people to Jesus through his preaching. His name was Dwight Lyman Moody.

Morgan closes his chapter on Andrew by stating: "We close our meditation by reminding ourselves that Christ's first disciple was not Peter, but Andrew, and the first need of the Lord is still the strong, quiet soul who is content to remain largely out of sight. By saying this I am not undervaluing Peter. I am not undervaluing any man who in the Divine will is put in the forefront; but I am attempting to emphasize the fact that if the kingdom of God had only the men whom we sometimes designate leaders, the work would suffer. It is by the host of those who, like Andrew are strong, cautious, and faithful, that work will be accomplished."[34]

At least a year later, Jesus calls Andrew and Peter to leave their fishing enterprise and come after Him and fish for men. These men were true fishermen and made their livelihood from this profession. It is interesting that the word for net in Matthew 4:18 is *amphiblestron*, which is close to our word amphibious, which is something that is related to both land and water, as they would throw the net in the water then drag it back to shore.[35]

Jesus told Andrew and his brother Peter to do two things—follow Him and fish for men. I love this analogy of fishing for men that Jesus gives. One of the basic principles in fishing is that you will never catch fish unless you go fishing. Another principle is at times you will fish but not catch anything. I have only been fishing a few times in my life, but I do enjoy it when I go, and I especially enjoy it when I catch fish.

Real fishermen will tell you, however, that though it certainly is fun to catch, the real joy is just being able to get out there and try. It reminds me of a statement Bobby Welch made. Bobby served for years as the pastor of First Baptist Church, Daytona Beach, Florida, and is the author of the FAITH Evangelism Program. He said, "We must teach our people to enjoy fishing as much as they love catching."

There are two simple points I wish to make in this chapter taken from the words of Jesus to Andrew—Follow Jesus, and Fish for Men.

Follow Jesus

"As he was walking along the Sea of Galilee, he saw two brothers, Simon (who is called Peter), and his brother Andrew. They were casting a net into the sea—for they were fishermen."

—MATTHEW 4:18

Jesus calls these fishermen, Peter, Andrew, and later James and John to leave their profession of fishing for a different task of fishing for souls. The word "follow" means to go after, to mimic, and to come.

One writer explains the word this way, "The command, Follow Me (in the Greek an adverb of place expressing a command), literally means 'come here.' The term after is used in the original to show the place they are to come: 'Your place is following after Me.'"[36]

I love the quick reaction of Peter, Andrew, James, and John—they immediately left their fishing for fish and followed Jesus, so they could begin fishing for souls.

"Immediately they left their nets and followed him."

—MATTHEW 4: 20

"Immediately they left the boat and their father and followed him."

—MATTHEW 4:22)

What does it mean for you to follow Jesus? You cannot follow Him physically as the original disciples did, but you can still follow Him. We follow Him by emulating His example in Scripture; we follow Him by praying to Him and reading His Word and obeying what the Spirit of God tells us.

I have yet to meet someone who is fishing for men and leading people to Jesus who is not following Jesus.

When I was teaching evangelism at Southeastern Baptist

Theological Seminary in Wake Forest, North Carolina, this truth became evident to me. Hannah was only about six or seven, and Bryant four or five. One day as we were driving home, we passed by this huge, ornate Buddhist Temple. Hannah asked me, "Dad, what is that?" I told her and she asked, "Do they love Jesus?" And I said, "Not like we do," and thought that was it. She then said, "Let us go tell them."

I wish I had been following the Lord more closely or I would not have said what I said. I said, "No, we are going home."

A little way down the road, she asked me again, "Can we go tell them?" and I said, "No." Then she asked, "Dad, why will you not tell them?"

I just got upset for a few miles, then the Lord convicted me. So I turned around my two-door Toyota Tercel, went back to the temple and sat in my car with this nervous look on my face. Hannah said, "Dad, you can stay here and I will go tell them about Jesus!"

We went and I shared with the monk and he gave us a tour of the temple.

Here is a tough statement, but it is so true and needs to be stated. If you are not fishing, then you are not following Jesus. It does not matter how many Bible studies or worship services or prayer meetings you attend, if you are not speaking to others about Christ, you are out of fellowship with the Lord. This is true for church staff, teachers, deacons, everybody.

FISH FOR MEN

"'Follow me,' he told them, 'and I will make you fish for people" (Matthew 4:19). Notice the part of this verse that says, "And I will make you fish for people." Evangelism is not so much what we do for God but what God does through us. Jesus says, "I will make you fish for people." He takes the divine initiative and uses us to tell others His good news.

The best definition of evangelism I ever came across was Bill Bright's from Campus Crusade for Christ. "Evangelism is sharing the Gospel in the power of the Holy Spirit and leaving the results to God." Another good definition is the one given by D. T. Niles, "Evangelism is one beggar telling another beggar where to find bread."

From Andrew's life and example I am challenged with this thought—we will tell people about Jesus as a result of spending time with Jesus.

Would it not be a wonderful thing if you and I followed Jesus with such passion and intimacy that we never missed an opportunity to brag on our Lord and actually give a verbal witness for Christ?

I would love to be where James Harper was in his walk with Christ. Perhaps Harper would define evangelism or witnessing as one drowning man telling another how to get to safety. Harper was saved when he was fourteen years old and called to preach when he was seventeen. He served a little church that had twenty people and it grew to five hundred people in thirteen years. His wife passed away, but they had one daughter named Anna. He and his daughter and her cousin were on a ship from England to visit America and Harper was to preach at the Moody Church in Chicago. However, the name of the ship was the Titanic. James Harper, along with most of the men, died in the icy waters of the Atlantic, but Anna and her cousin were rescued.

Years later a Scotsman who was also on the ship, but who survived, told this story about Harper. This man told how he clung to a piece of wood for survival and a wave brought Harper close to him and Harper asked him "Sir, are you saved?" And the Scotsman said, "No, I am not.

Later Harper came by again and asked him, "Are you saved now?!"

The response was the same. So Harper shared Acts 16:31 with the man, "Believe on the Lord Jesus Christ and you will be saved."

The man believed and was saved, and he thus became James Harper's last convert.

I want to be like John Harper. I want to be so close to Jesus that whether I am experiencing good times or bad, good health or ill, or on the brink of death, to be so closely following Jesus that I tell others about Jesus.

Andrew was the first of the twelve disciples chosen by Christ. And when we encounter him in the New Testament he is bringing someone to Christ. **The only way he could do this was by being so close to Jesus he shared out of the overflow of his relationship with Christ.**

This is still true for you and me today. The only way we can be good fishers of men is that we must be following Jesus, mimicking Him, walking with Him.

I am convinced that the main reason the average church member today does not share is a *followship* problem. I hear these statistics, that more than ninety percent of church members will not share their faith and that fifty-four percent of pastors in a six-month time frame did not witness to anyone. We have many clergy and laypeople that need either to meet Christ or really start following Him.

Jesus put it best, "Follow Me, and I will make you fish for people."

David Platt's book, *Radical: Taking Back Your Faith from the American Dream*, is very powerful and convicting. He writes clearly about our purpose in life—we are blessed by God to be a blessing to others, and every Christian's job is the Great Commission.

Some quotes that stood out to me from Platt's book are these:

"Enjoy His grace, extend His glory."

"It's a foundational truth: God creates, blesses, and saves each of us for a radically global purpose."

"Indeed, Jesus Himself has not merely called us to go to all nations; He has created us and commanded us to go to all nations."

"We have unnecessarily (and unbiblically) drawn a line of distinction, assigning the obligations of Christianity to a few while keeping the privileges of Christianity for us all...Every saved person this side of heaven owes the gospel to every lost person this side of hell."[37]

I encourage you to be like Andrew and follow after Jesus so passionately that you take advantage of every opportunity God grants to you to fish for people, or lead them to Christ. You can do it!

FOR
THE
ONE

CHAPTER 5

THE SAMARITAN WOMAN

Jesus said,

"Everyone who drinks from this water
will get thirsty again. But whoever drinks from the water
that I will give him will never get thirsty again.
In fact, the water I will give him will become a well of water
springing up in him for eternal life."

JOHN 4:13-14

I listened recently to Dr. Russell Moore, executive director of the Southern Baptist Convention's Ethics & Religious Liberty Commission. On his podcast he shared the true story of when he was a little boy in Mississippi. The Sunday school teacher scolded him for putting a quarter in his mouth and she said, "You do not know where that quarter has been; it could have been in a colored man's hand." That is so very sad. Dr. Moore said they also hypocritically sang this song, "Jesus loves the little children, all the children of the world, red and yellow, black and white, they are precious in His sight."

Jesus loved and loves all people. When you read the New Testament, you read of how He gave value to everyone He met—

the rich and poor, those of different gender, race, backgrounds; He loved all people and died for the sins of all that we might be forgiven and live eternally with Him.

Three things come to my mind regarding the blessings that are ours as we study the Master:

1. We have the privilege of studying the greatest Person who ever lived.

2. We get the opportunity to study God's Word. We do not take that for granted. There are those all over this world who absolutely love what we get to do every day and every Sunday; we get to open, read, and dive into the Holy Scriptures.

3. We position ourselves to be greatly blessed, because in learning about Jesus we can then go and do what He did. As a result, we will live a life that blesses others and we too will be blessed.

John 4 is one of the great texts that deals with Jesus' ministry to the "one." It is a powerful account of how Christ engaged in dialogue with a person who was a different gender and race than him, as well as one who held different theological convictions. It is a masterful example from which we can learn a great deal.

The longest dialogue recorded in the Bible between Jesus and another human being is found in John 4. It is so interesting to me that this conversation was with a woman, and a dreaded Samaritan at that! But Jesus did not show prejudice or discriminate against people. He knew that everyone needed help and needed to be restored to the God who created them.

Jesus steered a conversation with her and reached out to her because He cared for her soul. He loved all people, spoke to all people, and offered hope to all.

Like many people in our country today, this woman had a

religious knowledge or background but was not practicing her religion. G. Campbell Morgan writes, "She presents the picture of the condition of thousands of people today. They have a religious background, perchance some problem dismissed, and it may be some hope accepted, but having no practical bearing on life." [38] Or as a man once told me, he was a member of the largest church in America—a non-practicing Catholic.

JOHN 4:1-15

Notice in John 4:4 that Jesus needed to go through Samaria. Most Jews did not take this route as they traveled from the southern part of Israel or Judah to the northern part to Galilee. They would travel east across the Jordan River and then north, taking a longer, more circuitous route instead of the easier direct route through Samaria. The reason for this was the hostility between the Jews and Samaritans. Part of that hostility can be detected in the woman's voice.

In John 4:6, Jesus meets this woman at Jacob's well. The reason He stops at the well is to get some water, as He is thirsty from His travels.

Borchert tells, "The journey for Jesus obviously had been a tiring experience, and the text indicates that being exhausted, he sat down by or at (*epi*) the well about the sixth hour. The time notation "the sixth hour," if reckoned from 6:00am would mean that it was about noon—the period of the day in the Mediterranean world when it is hot and people are ready for their siesta break. It certainly was not the time for doing rough tasks like hauling water. But if the time were taken according to the Roman time pattern from midnight or noon, it would be either six o'clock in the morning or evening, not illogical times for fetching water." [39]

This well was located at the foot of Mount Gerizim, the center of worship for the Samaritans. I believe the sixth hour refers to noon. It was not a popular time to come to the well. Perhaps the woman came because there was a need for water or maybe she came because she knew there would not be many people at this time of day and she wished to avoid people because of her past.[40]

If this is the case, then later in the chapter her willingness to speak and testify to the men in John 4:28-29 is even more impressive.

Jesus initiated the conversation in John 4:7. Had He waited for her to talk to Him they never would have had the conversation. He did not ask her a question; He asked a favor from her, a drink of water.

Jesus knew who she was. She was a Samaritan woman and she was not a moral individual. She had a past with many skeletons in her closet. She had been married five times and now was living with a man who was not her husband (John 4:17-18). She was an adulterer and a fornicator. Jesus loved the sinner but not the sin.

And she was startled that Jesus, being a Jew, would speak to her, a Samaritan woman. I like the way Tenney describes the scene in John 4:9, "There was a trace of sarcasm in the woman's reply, as if she meant, 'We Samaritans are the dirt under your feet until you want something; then we are good enough!' Jesus paid no attention to her flippancy or to her bitterness. He was more interested in winning the woman than in winning an argument."[41]

The Samaritan woman makes an interesting and insightful statement in verse 9, that Jews have no dealings with the Samaritans. For the most part that was true, but Jesus was not like the others. Why did the two races have no dealings with one another? It goes back to their histories. Solomon's son, Rehoboam, remained in Jerusalem with the tribes of Judah and Benjamin, and Jeroboam, Solomon's servant, son of Nebat, fled to Ephraim with the other ten tribes and made Shechem, located just south of Samaria, his capital. The twelve tribes of Israel, the nation as a whole, was fractured.

They were prevented a civil war because God intervened in 1 Kings 12:24. Jeroboam was an evil man and led the people astray in 1 Kings 12:25-29. For some more history, move forward to 722 BC, when the king of Assyria, Sargon, came and destroyed Israel and its capital, Samaria. He deported the captives to Assyria and replaced them with foreigners who intermarried with the remaining Jews, thus the name "half-breeds."

Signs of disharmony are first seen in 537 BC, when the Jews returned from the Babylonian Captivity. They would not accept help from the Samaritans in the rebuilding of the temple in Jerusalem (Ezra 4:1-2).[42]

The governor of Samaria at that time was a man mentioned in Nehemiah named Sanballat. He built a temple in Samaria on Mount Gerizim to rival the one in Jerusalem. The Samaritan woman refers to Mount Gerizim in John 4:20 when she says, "this mountain."[43]

Jesus approached her with a simple, common request, that she give Him a drink of water (John 4:7). It was conversation starter. Again, it was profound that Jesus spoke to this woman because He was a man and a Jew, and she was a woman and a Samaritan.

Jesus speaks to her about a different kind of water in John 4:10, living water. She is perhaps still thinking on the physical level, thinking that the living water Jesus is talking about is fresh drinking water. The well where they are is deep indeed, as the woman asserts in verse 11. Today, after having been covered through the years with debris, the well is still 75 feet.[44]

The Samaritan woman's reference to "our father Jacob" in John 4:12 was perhaps a way of affirming her people, the Samaritans, in the eyes of Jesus, who was a Jew.[45] You can tell there is some barb or bite in her defensive comments.

Look at what Jesus says to her in John 4:13-14, "Everyone who drinks from this water will get thirsty again. But whoever drinks from the water that I will give him will never get thirsty again. In fact, the water I will give him will become a well of water springing up in him for eternal life."

Jesus makes it crystal clear to her that He is not talking about H2O! Rather, He is speaking about the Holy Spirit.

"'The one who believes in me, as the Scripture has said, will have streams of living water flow from deep within him.' He said this about the Spirit. Those who believed in Jesus were going to receive the Spirit, for the Spirit had not yet been given because Jesus had not yet been glorified" (John 7:38-39).

"This inner spring contrasts with the water from the well, which required hard work to acquire. Jesus was speaking of the Holy Spirit who brings salvation to a person who believes and through Him offers salvation to others."[46]

If you know the Lord Jesus, does John 4:14 describe your life? Note the words "springing up." It connotes the idea of bubbling over, a life of real joy, spiritual satisfaction. Jesus lived this life and offers it to us. One of the ways this bubbling of joy happens is we consistently share Christ with others.

Fish writes, "Jesus moved naturally from the physical to the spiritual. This is the secret of a good approach in witnessing for Him. Move almost effortlessly from the material to the spiritual. Today the mind of men is thinking in the realm of the secular, the material. You want to build a bridge between the secular and the spiritual."

Jesus began bridging the physical and spiritual in John 4:10 with the words, "if you knew." These were powerful words. If she knew that the very Creator of the Universe was speaking to her, she would have fallen on her face and worshipped Him and asked for eternal life.

Jesus was the Master witness. We can learn so much by studying His example. And the other way we learn to approach people and speak to them about Jesus is just do it.

While in Dallas at our Southern Baptists of Texas board meeting, we went on a dinner boat cruise on Lake Grapevine. I prayed before we left for an opportunity to witness to someone. God gave me three people to share with, the captain and two of his helpers!

I have a word for you, as ambassadors for Christ here on earth, we are spiritual interjectors. By that I mean we move from the earthly, mundane level in our conversations to the holy and spiritual. The more that we witness, the better we become at doing this. We should always be reading and learning how we can better engage people with the Gospel.

The Samaritan woman has a void in her life that only Jesus can satisfy and fulfill. She has a spiritual hunger and thirst that only Jesus can satiate. She is representative of all lost people— they hunger and thirst for spiritual reality. Augustine said there is a spiritual vacuum in every soul placed there by God that only He can fill. In John 4:15, she asked Jesus to give her this living water.

Perhaps you can relate to this woman. Maybe you also have a shady past and the skeletons in your closet rattle noisily in your life, bringing you shame and grief. The way to deal with this is give Jesus your past, present, and future. He will silence the skeletons and give you new life.

Three truths that we learn in John 4 from Jesus and His encounter with the Samaritan woman are that we need to love all people, talk to all people, and give hope to all people. Jesus is the perfect role model.

1. LOVE ALL PEOPLE.

Red, and yellow, and black and white, they are all indeed precious in His sight. I pastor a racially diverse congregation. It is not the color of your skin that matters to us. We love all peoples and desire for all nations to know Christ and experience eternal life. We need to follow the example of Christ and not let any pride or prejudice or anything else hinder us in presenting the Gospel to everyone...Notice the difference in approaches that Jesus utilized with this woman and with Nicodemus in John 3. The two individuals were vastly different. Nicodemus was a religious leader of the Jews, an educated and perhaps wealthy man, and a man of sound moral values. The woman in John 4 was a Samaritan who did not come to Jesus seeking religious insight, as did Nicodemus. She lacked the moral fortitude that characterized the life of Nicodemus.

"The Samaritan woman contrasts sharply with Nicodemus. He was seeking; she was indifferent. He was a respected ruler; she was an outcast. He was serious; she was flippant. He was a Jew; she was a despised Samaritan. He was (presumably) moral; she was immoral. He was orthodox; she was heterodox. He was learned in religious matters; she was ignorant. Yet in spite of all the differences between this "churchman" and this woman of the world, they both needed to be born again. Both had needs only Christ could meet."[47]

The two were very different and so was the approach that Jesus employed in witnessing to them. We need to keep in mind that everyone is different. While we give witness to one Gospel, there are many ways to go about presenting that Gospel. Theology remains the same, but our methodology is fluid and flexible. We shape our methods based on who that person is and how the Holy Spirit guides us.

Our church is located in the zip code 78759, one of the

most educated and affluent areas in our country. There is a vast difference, however, in the people who make up this zip code—some are very educated and affluent, while others are very poor and uneducated. Though the people are different and come from various socio-economic backgrounds, they are still people who need the Lord Jesus. We must reach out to the down and out, those like the Samaritan lady, and also the up and out, people like Nicodemus.

Part of being a missional church is to love all, show no partiality, and take the gospel to all. From Austin to Africa, from Texas to Tijuana—it is imperative to follow the example and commandment of Jesus and shine the Light of Truth to all.

2. TALK TO ALL PEOPLE.

Note that Jesus was not too tired or occupied to share with this woman. We often get preoccupied with our own needs or troubles and maybe even physically exhausted. When this happens, we look inward and do not have time for others. Allow me to ask you, as well as myself, a hard question—**how much has to be going right in your life before you will share Christ with someone else?**

Most of the time when we are tired or discouraged, we pass on opportunities to share the love of God. In actuality that is such a wonderful time to do so because that way people can actually see our Christianity at work. This is convicting for me if not for anyone else. I must constantly be reminded that I am here for God's glory and not my own glory or comfort. I am always on mission with God, whether I am oversees on a mission trip or talking to someone at a local gas station. I really enjoy being alone, and that is okay at times, but we must always be sensitive to those around us who need us to love and share.

Some Christians argue that they will just live good moral

lives, and that will be their witness. However, people may think you are a Muslim or Buddhist or a good and moral atheist. But when you open your mouth and give testimony to Jesus Christ, that erases all doubt. Just "living a good moral life" is not the method of Jesus. Jesus spoke to people.

3. OFFER HOPE TO ALL PEOPLE.

You and I have the Holy Spirit living in us and we have the cure to the cancer of the soul called sin. Our job is to love people and offer them Jesus. One of the neat ways to do this is by offering to pray with people, as that will help open up conversations. And then let the Holy Spirit use you and help you. There are multiple ways to present the Gospel, whether through reading from a Bible as the Gideons do or sharing a gospel tract like Steps to Peace with God or The Five Crosses that I wrote. You can also download the One Cross app. There are so many ways. We have many ways; we just need people to share!!

I had a text recently from my friend, Tom: "On the Texas A&M Kingsville campus. The Lord is providing lots of opportunities to engage the students in conversations with several giving their lives to the Lord. Thanks for your prayers. Remain blessed."

Jesus loved all people as John 3:16 tells us and His life shows us; He spoke to everyone and showed no discrimination and He gave hope when there was no hope.

JOHN 4:16-26

This Samaritan woman, like Hagar in Genesis 16 and Rahab the harlot in Joshua 2, had a tough past. These women had made mistakes and yet they found in God the God who loves and forgives. No one is beyond the reach of God's saving arm.

Jesus went directly to the Samaritan woman's insufficiency and instructed her in what she needed to do. He told her the good news about everlasting life and living water; now He will tell her the bad news in John 4:16. The bad news is this—you have sinned against God. He did not use those exact words, but she got the message when He told her to go get her husband. It was not proper etiquette for her to be talking to a stranger without her husband,[48] so, Jesus told her to go get him but He also told her this for another reason, and that was to reveal her need.

In John 4:17-18, Jesus told her something that only He could know. She had been married five times, and I gather from verse 18 that she is sleeping with a man but he is not her husband. Jesus went there. Yes, He confronted her in her sin and yet He also commended her for her honesty.

This woman was amazed that He knew this about her because they had only met that day at noon! Because of this, we learn in John 4:19, she assumed that He was a prophet.

In verse 20, she tries to divert the conversation about her sin to a theological argument. She cleverly attempts to steer this conversation away from her sin to an old doctrinal debate, but Jesus would not take the bait.

She tried to draw Jesus into the controversy between the Jews and the Samaritans as to the proper place of worship. The Samaritans liked to remind others that Abraham first built an altar to God in nearby Shechem in Genesis 12:6-7. The Samaritans did not accept all of the Old Testament, but only the first five books known as the Torah or Pentateuch. The Jews, however, accepted all of the Old Testament.

Second Chronicles 6:6 tells us that the city of choice for the temple is Jerusalem.[49] "But I have chosen Jerusalem, so that My name may be there, and I have chosen David to be over My people Israel."

The Samaritans pointed out how Moses instructed the people so that they set up an altar on Mount Ebal. The tribes were divided into two camps—one at Mount Gerizim, proclaiming the blessings of God, and the other half on Mount Ebal, pronouncing the curses of God on account of sin (Deuteronomy 27:1-28:68).[50]

"The Jews held that since Solomon had been commissioned to build the temple in Jerusalem, the center of worship would be located there. The controversy was endless, and Jesus did not intend to allow Himself to be drawn into a futile discussion."[51]

Jesus broadens the way the Samaritan woman thinks about worship. "Jesus told her, 'Believe me, woman, an hour is coming when you will worship the Father neither on this mountain nor in Jerusalem.'"

This is a prophetic word, because she will believe on Christ and not worship Him on Mount Gerizim or Jerusalem.

Also, in AD 70 the temple at Jerusalem will be destroyed and thousands of Samaritans will be killed on Mount Gerizim. As MacArthur writes, "More significantly, the new covenant renders all external ceremonies and rituals, whether Jewish or Samaritan, obsolete."[52]

In John 4:22, Jesus further instructs her by telling her that she worshipped what she did not know. This is perhaps a reference to the syncretistic worship of the Samaritans, as they combined the worship of God with other foreign deities.[53] Salvation is of the Jews, Jesus told her. He is the Messiah and Author of salvation and He came from the Jews, from David's lineage of the tribe of Judah.

Jesus gives this woman truths and instructs her about proper worship in John 4:23-24. When He says, "the hour is coming, and now is," I believe He is referring to the fact that He is present in this world and He will change the way worship takes place.

God is Spirit and He desires all to worship Him in spirit and truth. This is a wonderful word of instruction on Christian worship. God is not a material substance. He cannot be represented by some idol.[54] He is Spirit; He is everywhere at all times. He desires those who will recognize Him as such and will worship Him in spirit and truth.

John Piper says in *Desiring God* that worship is to be an affair of the heart. And we are to worship in truth; worship is to be an affair of the head. We are to worship God with all that we have, with our emotions and our intellects—in spirit and truth.

Jesus said in Matthew 22:37, quoting the Shema in Deuteronomy 6, that you are to "love the LORD your God with all your heart, with all your soul, and with all your mind."

In John 4:25, the woman shares her hope in the Messiah who would come. Perhaps as Jesus spoke, it made her think of the Messiah, and we know why! He was the Messiah.

God's ways and thoughts are so much higher and holier than our own, are they not? "'For my thoughts are not your thoughts, and your ways are not my ways.' This is the Lord's declaration. 'For as heaven is higher than earth, so my ways are higher than your ways, and my thoughts than your thoughts'" (Isaiah 55:8-9).

Here is the Messiah sitting at a well in Samaria talking to a sinful and searching woman! Amazing. Before I met Christ, I was a sinful and searching man.

"The Samaritans expected a coming messianic leader. But they did not expect Him to be an anointed king of the Davidic line, since they rejected all the Old Testament except the Pentateuch. Based on Deuteronomy 18:15–18, they expected a Moses-like figure who would solve all their problems.

The Samaritan woman now understood a part of what Jesus said. She wistfully longed for the messianic days when the Messiah would explain everything."[55]

Jesus tells her that He is that very Messiah. "Jesus told her, 'I, the one speaking to you, am he.'"

"In response to her reply, Jesus immediately seized the opportunity and declared (lit.), "I am [ego eimi; 4:26], the one speaking to you." In John the use of ego eimi is an important theological theme that is used in the mouth of Jesus as a self-identifying vehicle for announcing some important theological idea concerning him. Normally the expression is accompanied by some thematic description such as "bread of life" (6:35), "light of the world" (8:12), "door of the sheep" (10:7), "good shepherd" (10:14), or "resurrection and life" (11:25). But in a few places like the present one ego eimi is used without such an accompanying description (cf. also 6:20; 8:58; 18:5)."[56]

WHAT LESSONS CAN WE LEARN FROM JESUS AS HE TALKS WITH THE SAMARITAN WOMAN?

1. SHARE THE GOOD NEWS AND THE BAD NEWS.

The good news is the living water that God offers all who believe. The Holy Spirit comes into us the moment we turn from sin and embrace Jesus as our personal Savior and Lord. That is wonderful news indeed! So what is the bad news? The bad news is we are sinners. It is true but still hard for people to hear. Jesus told this woman clearly that she had lived and was living a life of sin.

2. BE WINSOME AND KIND IN YOUR WITNESS FOR CHRIST.

Please do not overlook this—we must always be kind and affirm what we can affirm in people. Everyone needs words of encouragement, yes even those without Christ, who are living in sin. A major lesson I learned from Dave Kinnaman's book, *Unchurched*, is that we, as believers, need to be more kind and forgiving and reach out to people in love!

3. KEEP THE CONVERSATION FOCUSED ON THE GOSPEL, NOT THEOLOGICAL ARGUMENTS.

I think it is okay to do apologetics, but let us learn from the Master Himself. He spoke to the debate, but did not get sidetracked and drawn into the vortex of winning the argument. Our job is not to win arguments but to help lead hurting souls to Jesus.

4. BE BOLD!

Jesus, in John 4:26, was bold and very truthful. I read with much interest another For the One testimony from one of our church members. It was from a lady who has been living the Christian life before her colleagues and bosses. She thinks she is the only Christian, at least in her sphere of people at work. She thought she was in trouble when her CEO called her in. Instead, the CEO told her what a great job she was doing. He is an agnostic and does not believe in prayer. He asked her, "Do you pray a lot?" and she said she prays about everything and that she and her husband had even prayed if she would take this job! This Christian lady shared with him the very specific things she was praying for. A few days later he commended her for the good work she was doing in her job and said, "Keep praying for me."

I read the story again this week of how a Christian man a few years ago witnessed to the atheist magician and performer Penn Jillette. It really is a fascinating and true story. He actually made a YouTube video about how a Christian businessman approached him after a show in Vegas and spoke to him and gave him a Bible. Jillette said, "I don't respect people who don't proselytize. I don't respect that at all. If you believe that there's a heaven and hell and people could be going to hell or not getting eternal life or whatever, and you think that it's not really worth telling them because it would make it socially awkward…How much do you have to hate someone to believe that everlasting life is possible and not tell them that?"[57]

For Jesus, His life consisted of pleasing the Father and the Father's will was for Jesus to come and serve and die for the sins of the world. As His followers today our mission is the same as that of Jesus, we live for God and pour out our lives in service to Him and in so doing we are blessed beyond measure.

JOHN 4:27-42

As we look at John 4:27-42, we see the disciples' perplexity, the Samaritan woman's proclamation, the Lord's preaching, and the Samaritans' persuasion.

THE DISCIPLES WERE PERPLEXED (JOHN 4:27-33)

The disciples returned from buying food in the city and they marveled at the fact that Jesus was speaking to a Samaritan woman. However, they dared not ask Him why He was doing that. Perhaps they had learned enough by now to know that the Lord knew what He was doing, and He did not need to answer to them but they to Him.

D. A. Carson states, "Their unvoiced surprise that he was talking with a Samaritan woman reflects the prejudices of the day. Some (though by no means all) Jewish thought held that for a rabbi to talk much with a woman, even his own wife, was at best a waste of time and at worst a diversion from the study of Torah, and therefore potentially a great evil that could lead to Gehenna, hell (Pirke Aboth 1:5). Some rabbis went so far as to suggest that to provide their daughters with knowledge of the Torah was as inappropriate as to teach them lechery, i.e. to sell them into prostitution (Mishnah Sotah 3:4; the same passage also provides the contrary view). Add to this the fact that this woman was a Samaritan...; and the disciples' surprise is understandable. Jesus himself was not hostage to the sexism of his day."[58]

In verse 31, the disciples were concerned about Jesus' eating. Can you imagine their confusion when He told them in verse 32, "I have food to eat of which you do not know." They perhaps looked at one another with a confused look on their faces and asked, "Has anyone brought Him anything to eat?" (John 4:33). Someone said that with Jesus, school was always in session with the disciples. Jesus spent time with them and was available to teach them spiritual lessons. They were slow to learn and understand at times, but the Lord was patient with them and carefully instructed them regarding the deeper truths.

The way the disciples would turn the world upside for Christ was rooted in this ingenious discipleship move of Jesus. He meticulously trained them in the deeper things of God, both by precept and example.

THE SAMARITAN WOMAN PROCLAIMED (JOHN 4:28-29, 39)

This woman wasted no time in telling others what she had heard and experienced in Jesus Christ. Note in verse 28, she left her water pot; that is very interesting is it not? The very reason she went to the well was to obtain water but she had received different, more satisfying water, spiritual water, and she was a changed lady. After she met Christ her priorities changed. Her main mission was to tell others what she had experienced. And note she spoke to the men. She was not intimidated nor did she allow social laws to dictate to her with whom she could speak.

She spoke to the leaders of the city and perhaps she knew that if they heard her they might believe and if the men believed, then the families could be brought to faith as well.

In John 4:29, she tells the men the miraculous event of Jesus telling her about her past. This is no doubt a reference to the Lord's words to her in verse 18.

"In her joy of discovery she forgot her water jar. It was more important to her now to share her new faith. Her words A Man who told me everything I ever did, were bound to stir interest. Perhaps in that village some who heard her had been partners in her past life. Perhaps they wondered, *Could this One also know about us?*"[59]

We are in great need of men and women in the church today who will not be embarrassed or intimidated, but go and tell everyone what Jesus Christ has done for them.

Pastor Paul Harris in Mineral Wells, Texas, told me about Greg Ivey. Paul would go to prison and share Christ and disciple some of the men who had received Christ. Greg was serving a sentence for his crimes and would end up serving over 20 years. He was one of the more resistant prisoners. Also, Paul said the material seemed to go over his head. But a couple of years ago when he was released from prison, he hand-copied the discipleship book, *Charting a Bold Course*, and get this, he has discipled 200 men! He has a ministry today called Con for Christ where he helps ex-cons get jobs. He started his own construction company. Paul kept telling me that Greg Ivey is the real deal.

Don't give up on people. You never know the impact you are making and the difference God can make in a person's life. I am sure no one ever imagined this Samaritan lady would be so used by God and become a great evangelist for Jesus! No one may have ever imagined Greg Ivey would do such great things for God, either, but look what God did.

JESUS PREACHED (JOHN 4:32-38, 41)

Look at verses 32 and 34 as Jesus instructs the disciples. He tells His disciples about a food they do not know about. His food was to **do the will of the Father who sent Him and to finish His work.** And what was that will of the Father and the work to which He was sent? It was to save the world.

As followers of Jesus Christ, we too have this same spiritual food. It is to do the Father's will and participate in the work. It is God's will for every follower of Jesus to do His will and work. What is this, you ask? It is sharing the Gospel and leading people to Christ! As we share the good news of Jesus, it brings spiritual satisfaction and fulfillment far greater than the physical nourishment of food.

Why does Jesus compare sharing His life with this woman to spiritual food? There is a spiritual fulfillment and joy that comes from serving God that far exceeds any other kind of nourishment.

It is such a joy to read of how many in our church are partaking of this spiritual food of doing the Father's will and participating in the work. I read a For the One testimony from one of our Connect Group classes. They went to Dairy Queen after church and befriended a guy who was eating there. He had heard the Great Hills members talking about church, so he introduced himself to the group. They invited him to GHBC. He attended the Connect Group class and committed his life to Jesus during the worship service. I love what Charles Arnold wrote, "Even a bunch of seasoned citizens can reach out For the One!"

Jesus preached in John 4:35-38. I love verse 35. Some believe that as Jesus said, "Open your eyes and look at the fields, because they are ready for harvest" in John 4:35, that the Samaritans could be seen coming out of the town to meet Him. Jesus tells us to do away with delay and excuses and get busy. Satan will try all he can to prevent you and me from telling others about Jesus. Do not listen to him; be bold and plant the gospel seed.

In John 4:36-38, Jesus teaches the disciples about the importance of sowing and reaping. One will sow, the other will reap, but God gives the increase, as Paul stated:

"I planted, Apollos watered, but God gave the growth. So then neither the one who plants nor the one who waters is anything, but only God who gives the growth. Now he who plants and he who waters are one, and each will receive his own reward according to his own labor."

—1 CORINTHIANS 3:6-8

There is rejoicing among those who sow and reap as people are brought into the kingdom. "The reaper is already receiving pay and gathering fruit for eternal life, so that the sower and reaper can rejoice together" (John 4:36).

"Harvest time in the ancient world was a time of joy (Ruth 3:2, 7; Isaiah 9:3). There is also great joy at the time of salvation (cf. Luke 15:7, 10, 32). The disciples had the greater joy of seeing the completion of the process (John 4:38).

A sower has a harder time because he sees no immediate fulfillment. John the Baptist stirred a nation to repent, but he died before the day of Pentecost, when the disciples in great joy saw thousands come to faith in Jesus."[60]

John 4:37 says, "One sows and another reaps." Just as there will be no harvest for food unless one sows and another reaps, there will be no souls saved unless some plant the seed and others harvest. My friend at Liberty Theological Seminary, Dr. David Wheeler, says we live in an unseeded generation. What he means is the Gospel seed is not being sown and as a result we are not seeing more people saved. Most of the time we will sow the seed and that is okay, because in God's sovereign way and will,

He will take the seed that is sown and accomplish His perfect will. God will always do His part; we must be willing to do ours.

I believe Jesus is referring to reaping the spiritual harvest that is about to come from the Samaritans who will believe on Him in verse 38. He has labored and so has the Samaritan woman. Now the disciples get to reap. This teaching applies to us as well. There will be times that all we need to do is share because God has prepared the soil of their hearts as others have witnessed and proclaimed the Gospel. I love to see this principle in church where you and I are witnessing and inviting people to come to church. They come, hear the good news, and get saved; that is awesome.

There are times when God has so prepared the soil through others' witness that all we need to do is share and give the opportunity to pray to receive Christ and they will! If they are not ready they will tell you, but you do not know until you ask!

Jesus stayed two more days (John 4:40-41) and He preached to them and many more believed. He accomplished the Father's will for His life and finished the work He was sent to finish.

You may be wondering what God's will is for your life. I can tell you what it is. God's will and His work for your life are to tell people about Jesus and His salvation.

THE SAMARITANS WERE PERSUADED (JOHN 4:39-42)

The story ends in such a dramatic and wonderful way. Many of the Samaritans believed that Jesus is the Christ, the Savior of the world. Some believed because of the woman's testimony in verse 39. They are thrilled to meet Jesus and they invited Him to stay with them.

Verse 40 says that the Samaritans heard Jesus and asked Him to stay, a favorite word for John. It is the Greek word *meno*, meaning to abide or remain. The word is used 112 times in the New Testament, with 66 being in John's writings, 40 in the Gospel of John.

"Sometimes, as here, it means "to stay or dwell" in a place; a few times it means "to last or continue"; but more often it has a theological connotation: "to remain, continue, abide" (e.g., John 15:4–7)."[61]

John 4:41 says, "Many more believed."

According to John 4:42, the Samaritans said that many of them believed after they heard Jesus preach firsthand. The Apostle Paul understood the Father's will and work for His life, and he spent his life in service bringing many to Jesus. He writes in 2 Corinthians 5:11, "Knowing, therefore, the terror of the Lord, we persuade men."

Are people coming to faith in Christ because of your faithful and consistent testimony that you live before them and speak in their presence? Are you investing in people and inviting them to church so that they hear the gospel and are convicted and converted?

How many of you are persuaded that Jesus is indeed the Christ the Son of God and the Savior of the world? Many of you no doubt are convinced and you have fully committed your life to the Lord and you are walking with Him. Others need Christ in your life. You need to do as this woman did and as her fellow countrymen and give your life, loyalty, and allegiance to Jesus. He is indeed the Messiah, and today you can meet Him as your Lord and Savior. Believe on Him and turn from your sins.

FOR THE ONE

CHAPTER 6

THE APOSTLE PETER

"Don't be afraid," Jesus told Simon.
"From now on you will be catching people."
Then they brought the boats to land,
left everything, and followed him."

LUKE 5:10-11

When you study the life of the greatest person who ever lived, Jesus Christ, you notice in the Bible that He spent much time alone in prayer with the Father, but He also spent large amounts of time in the presence of others. He taught, healed, and helped the multitudes, but He poured His life into the twelve apostles, and especially into the lives of Peter, James, and John.

Here we focus in on how Jesus loved and ministered to one of His disciples, the Apostle Peter, who along with James and John made up the inner circle of three that our Lord spent most of His time with here on earth. I love the Apostle Peter. He was quite an individual.

I enjoy studying biographies and autobiographies; I believe it is a great way to not only learn but also better yourself. It is humbling and rewarding to study the great men and women of the past. I learn from their successes as well as their failures.

In John Boles biography on Thomas Jefferson, he gives a thorough description of the life and times of America's third president. We all leave our mark, and Thomas Jefferson left a big one. He is remembered most for these three things: author of the Declaration of Independence, a staunch supporter of religious liberty, and the founder of the University of Virginia.

Peter is one of the great trophies of God's grace, and he indeed left an indelible mark for the kingdom of God. You read about his life and ministry in the Gospels and the Book of Acts, as well as studying the two epistles he wrote. Many of us can see ourselves reflected in his life. **He is bold and yet cowardly; he is faithful and at times faithless; he often speaks his mind before thinking about what he is saying.** On one occasion he even pulls Jesus aside and rebukes Him!

Peter finishes well, which is important to remember. At Jesus' passion he denies the Lord, but after Christ appears to him in John 21 and restores him, we see a mighty transformation in Peter. At Pentecost he stands and preaches, and three thousand people are saved in Acts 2, and five thousand men in Acts 3!

How is a man like that made? Jesus patiently shaped, disciplined, and chiseled this hot-tempered man from a chunk of coal to a diamond. It did not happen overnight. Peter was difficult, exasperating, and stubborn, but he was worth the effort Jesus invested in him, as he became a champion and chief spokesperson for Christ and the church.

Peter was brought to Jesus by his brother Andrew in John 1:40-42. Jesus changes his name from Simon to Cephas, Petros, or Peter, which means stone. He was a rock for Christ. Along with James and John, Peter spent more time with Jesus than the others, and these three had the pristine honor of being present at the Lord's Transfiguration in Matthew 17.

G. Campbell Morgan calls Peter the greatest human who ever lived. He was a man of powerful intellect and emotion. He asks more questions than any of the other disciples. [62] He asks the following questions: To whom shall we go? How often shall my brother betray me and I forgive him? What shall this man do?

As for intensity and passionate emotion, you can detect it in his voice when he says, "Depart from me, for I am a sinful man, O Lord!" (Luke 5:8). When he told Jesus that he should not go to the cross, when he tells Christ that he will lay down his life for Him, when he asks if he can come to Jesus on the water, when he tells the other disciples that he is going back to fishing, and in John 13:8-9, as Jesus washes his feet and he cries out, "Not my feet only but my hands and my head!"

Morgan also says Peter "lacked preciousness"; by that he means he lacked the ability to weld together all his elements of personality into strength, which resulted in him being a "trial to his friends, notwithstanding their love of him; and further, he was certainly a trial to himself." [63]

But Jesus can take and change and mold even the most powerful of men, those who are full of strong will and themselves. God can take them and change them and use them for His glory and kingdom purposes.

LOOK AT SOME OF THE ENCOUNTERS JESUS HAD WITH SIMON PETER—

1. LUKE 5:1-11

Here is an in-depth account of when Jesus called Peter, Andrew, James and John and invited them to follow Him so that they would be fishers of men (see Matthew 4:18-22). Walter

Liefeld, in his commentary on Luke, says this incident is not to be viewed separately from the accounts in Matthew and Mark 1:16-20. Liefeld writes, "Luke focuses on Peter, shows the sovereignty and holiness of Jesus in a way Matthew and Mark do not, and alone mentions the total abandonment of the disciples' possessions as an act of discipleship." [64] This is found in Luke 14:33.

Again, we see Peter at his best and worst. He offers to correct Jesus mildly in Luke 5:5, but then follows it up quickly with the refrain, "Nevertheless at Your word I will let down the net."

2. MATTHEW 16:13-20

This is a text that reveals Peter making the confession, "Jesus is the Christ, the Son of the living God" in Caesarea Philippi, a place I have visited in Israel.

It was a very pagan site with many gods and goddesses, where some worshiped Molech in the past by offering their firstborn child by throwing them into the water.

Jesus tells Peter he is blessed because God has revealed this to him. Unfortunately, many have misunderstood this text and elevated Peter to the Pope and papacy that God never intended.

In 1 Peter 5:1, Peter simply refers to himself as a fellow elder or pastor. Matthew 16:18 is very instructive: "And I also say to you that you are Peter, and on this rock I will build my church, and the gates of Hades will not overpower it."

I like the way D.A. Carson interprets this text—"The text says nothing about Peter's successors, infallibility, or exclusive authority...e.g., after Peter's death, his 'successor' would have authority over a surviving apostle, John. What the New Testament does show is that Peter is the first to make this formal confession and that his prominence continues in the earliest years of the church (Acts 1-12). But he, along with John, can be sent by other apostles (Acts 8:14); and he is held accountable for his actions by the Jerusalem church (Acts 11:1-18); and rebuked by Paul (Galatians 2:11-14). He is, in short,...('first among equals,'); and on the foundation of such men (Ephesians 2:20), Jesus built His church." [65]

In Matthew 16:19, the binding and loosing is tied to the preaching of the gospel: "I will give you the keys of the kingdom of heaven, and whatever you bind on earth will have been bound in heaven, and whatever you loose on earth will have been loosed in heaven."

People are bound by the message Peter preached, not the messenger Peter. Those who hear and believe the Gospel are saved here and hereafter, and those who reject are likewise condemned to hell.

Again Carson is very helpful, "He [Peter] has no direct pipeline to heaven, still less do his decisions force heaven to comply; but he may be authoritative in binding and loosing because heaven has acted first (Acts 18:9,10). Those he ushers in or excludes have already been bound or loosed by God according to the gospel already revealed and which Peter, by confessing Jesus and the Messiah, has most clearly grasped." [66]

3. JOHN 21:15-19

Jesus questions Peter's love and loyalty to Himself three times in these verses, the same number of times that Peter denied Jesus. This is a most revealing and intimate conversation recorded for us by John.

"These" can refer to "love Me more than these men love Me," or "love Me more than you love these men," or "these" could refer to the boats, fishing, etc. I believe it is the first example, in light of Peter saying that, though all else turn away, he never would. In the questions of love Jesus uses *agape* the first two times, then *phileo* the third time.

Perhaps in light of Peter's fierce betrayal, Jesus is asking "Do you even love Me with a brotherly love?" The usage of *oida* in the first two instances for "know" refers to an intellectual knowledge of a fact, but the last time Peter uses "know" it is *ginosko*, and it means to know through experience. [67]

This is not an exhaustive list of dealings that Jesus had with Peter. He truly is one of the great men of history, and one that we can appreciate and relate to as well. Morgan says that at Pentecost Peter is welded together in his personality and therefore we can conclude that he is precious indeed. [68]

Peter was not perfect; none of us are. We read of where Paul rebukes him in Galatians 2 for his hypocrisy. Morgan concludes his chapter on Peter by stating that he was "a man of untiring energy, of unbending loyalty, an intellect supremely illuminated, an emotion completely yielded to his Lord, and a will that bore him onward in the pathway of fellowship." [69]

LET'S FOCUS ON SOME LESSONS FROM THE LIFE OF PETER—

1. AN UNGUARDED STRENGTH CAN BECOME A WEAKNESS.

Peter's quick mind and sharp tongue got him into trouble. Just as he can be bold and zealous in defending Jesus by cutting off Malchus's ear (John 18:10), he can also be equally tenacious in denying that he even knew Christ, as he did in the hour of Jesus' passion (Matthew 26:69-75). He can say with great conviction that Jesus is the Christ, the Son of the living God, and then he can, with the same tongue and within the same setting in Matthew 16, rebuke Jesus. "Peter took him aside and began to rebuke him, 'Oh no, Lord! This will never happen to you!'" (Matthew 16:22).

We should be on guard and humble with our strengths, because if unchecked, those same strengths can become obstacles and trip us up.

2. EVEN THE FINEST SAINTS MUST CONTINUE TO GROW IN GRACE.

Peter was a pillar in the New Testament church, as the first twelve chapters in the book of Acts demonstrate; however, he still struggled and needed to grow in grace and in sanctification. Twenty plus years from the events recorded in Acts 2-3, we read in Galatians 2:11-14 that Paul confronted Peter. Paul told Peter that he was being a hypocrite because he had fellowship with the Gentiles until the Jews arrived, and then he withdrew from them. Also, Peter compelled Gentiles to live as Jews, so Paul rebuked him and reminded him that men are not justified by works, but by faith in Jesus Christ. None of us ever arrive; we are all in process and should be growing closer to the Lord daily, but we will have setbacks.

3. TO ERR IS HUMAN AND TO FORGIVE IS INDEED DIVINE.

Peter erred, but Jesus forgave and restored him completely. Peter rebuked the Lord, he lacked faith at times, and he even denied Jesus and cursed that he did not know Him. Yet Jesus fully forgave and restored Peter in John 21. We see that God used him mightily in the Book of Acts and in the writing of his two epistles, which he wrote in AD 63-64, during Nero's reign.

Peter finished well; he died a martyr's death in the AD 60s under Emperor Nero. He was crucified upside down. Peter was not perfect, but he genuinely loved Christ and repented when he sinned, and God forgave and used him mightily up until his death.

4. WINNING SOULS FOR CHRIST IS THE PASSION IN LIFE FOR THE DEDICATED CHRISTIAN.

Peter shows us this in his life and teachings. We see him witnessing and preaching in the Book of Acts, and we have noted how thousands came to faith in Christ through his ministry. Peter wrote these words:

"But you are a chosen race, a royal priesthood, a holy nation, a people for his possession, so that you may proclaim the praises of the one who called you out of darkness into his marvelous light."

—I PETER 2:9

Peter was a unique man whom God used powerfully. May Peter's zeal and passion for Christ and sharing Him with others encourage and motivate you and me to be better witnesses for Christ.

Perhaps the Lord has spoken to you through this chapter on Peter and revealed to you that you are not passionate for the things of God because you do not know God. I invite you to give your life to Christ and repent and be converted. Or, like Peter, you may have sinned against God and turned your back on all you know is right. God is inviting you back to Him, to once again walk with Him. You may feel like you have done some sinful things, but I would say we all have. Even one of God's finest soldiers, the Apostle Peter, sinned egregiously, yet God forgave and restored him to even greater usage for the kingdom of God.

FOR
THE
ONE

CHAPTER 7

THE APOSTLE JOHN

"Going on from there, he saw two other brothers,
James the son of Zebedee, and his brother John.
They were in a boat with Zebedee their father,
preparing their nets, and he called them.
Immediately they left their boat and their father
and followed him."

—MATTHEW 4:21-22

When you study someone's life and model your life after theirs, you naturally take on their characteristics and their passion. You see this happening frequently in the business world, education, or in other professions. People find someone they admire, and they pattern their lives after their mentor in order to have the same impact as the one they follow.

John loved Jesus Christ. Jesus personally trained John to be the man and the great pastor that he would become.

I do not think there is a greater compliment than for someone to say of us what they said of Peter and John in Acts 4:13:

"When they observed the boldness of Peter and John and realized that they were uneducated and untrained men, they were amazed and recognized that they had been with Jesus."

How did they know? It was manifested in their lives, behavior, their speech, and all that they did. Oh, I wish the same could be said of us. James Leo Garrett was my professor in Systematic Theology at Southwestern Baptist Theological Seminary. He was the hardest professor I ever had. This man is in his nineties, and he is still going strong and writing and ministering today. He is a brilliant and genuinely humble man who greatly impacted me more for who he is than what he taught.

I have so much respect for him even though he almost killed me in class! They called him machine-gun Garrett because he lectured so fast. Dr. Garrett earned a bachelor's degree from Baylor University, a master's degree from Princeton, and his PhD from Harvard. All of that is impressive, but I remember, as a student at Southwestern, my impressions one evening at the Ft. Worth Convention Center as Luis Palau was preaching. During the invitation, there was Dr. Garrett standing at the front as a decision counselor! I give him the greatest compliment that I could ever give—Dr. Garrett reminds me of Jesus.

"Going on from there, he saw two other brothers, James the son of Zebedee, and his brother John. They were in a boat with Zebedee their father, preparing their nets, and he [Jesus] called them. Immediately they left the boat and their father and followed him."

—MATTHEW 4:21-22

Jesus is still calling men and women to a special place of service. He is calling men and women to leave their vocations and come and give their lives in service to Him. I want to be faithful and call out the called in our church.

G. Campbell Morgan's classic book, *The Great Physician*, is one of the great reads in Christian literature. I have referred to it often in this book. Morgan records fifty evangelistic encounters in this book. I highly recommend it to you, as arguably the best book ever written on the subject before us. Morgan tells how Jesus came and called him in 1886 when he was a teacher, "loving my work, teaching boys. There came a day when Jesus passed me at the desk, and said, 'Come after Me, and I will make you a teacher of men.' I have no hesitation in making that affirmation. He called for the consecration of a natural capacity to His business. That is exactly what He did with John. He asked for the dedication of the skill and ability he had in his earthly calling to the higher business of the Kingdom which He was bringing in."[70]

John is the disciple referred to as "the one Jesus loved." He is not mentioned by name in his Gospel.[71] His name means *"God is gracious."* He was a fisherman, as was his brother James, and also his fishing partners Andrew and Peter. His mother's name was Salome who was the sister of Mary, the mother of Jesus; therefore, John and Jesus were first cousins.

John was more of a thinker, a mystic, a poet, and a seer. We read of his profound thoughts in the Prologue of the Gospel of John in John chapter 1. And as a mystic, thinker, and poet, Morgan says John "was looking for the invisible, listening for the inaudible, questing for the intangible."[72]

"The next day, John was standing with two of his disciples. When he saw Jesus passing by, he said, 'Look the Lamb of God!'

The two disciples heard him say this and followed Jesus. When Jesus turned and noticed them following him, he asked them, 'What are you looking for?'

They said to him, 'Rabbi' (which means 'Teacher'), 'where are you staying?'

'Come and you'll see,' he replied. So they went and saw where he was staying, and they stayed with him that day. It was about four in the afternoon."

—JOHN 1:35-39

John and Andrew are the two disciples in this text. Jesus told him and Andrew to "come and see." John indeed saw Jesus and he records this very clearly in his first Epistle. In 1 John 1:1-3, John says "we have seen" three times.

Also, in the book of Revelation, John tells how he sees Jesus in Revelation 1:13-17. Verse 17 reads, "And when I saw Him, I fell at His feet as dead. But He laid His right hand on me, saying to me, 'Do not be afraid; I am the First and the Last.'"

While he was on the island of Patmos, Jesus tells John, "Come up here, and I will show you things which must take place after this" (Revelation 4:1).

John saw Jesus and his goal for writing his Gospel was that others might see Him as well. "Jesus performed many other signs in the presence of his disciples that are not written in this book. But these are written so that you may believe that Jesus is the Messiah, the Son of God, and that by believing you may have life in his name" (John 20:30-31).

John served as a pastor at the church of Ephesus from around AD 66-95. He was exiled to Patmos for preaching Christ in AD 95 and it was while he was on this island, really a rock quarry, that he received the Apocalypse, the Book of Revelation, from Jesus Christ.

John was the only one of the twelve Apostles who did not die a violent martyr's death, but his life was very difficult, as he was sentenced to serve at Patmos, a Roman penal colony for hardened criminals. I visited Patmos in July 2004 on a Sunday. There was a group of Christians worshiping in the place where John is believed to have written the Book of Revelation.

NOTICE SOME OF THE ENCOUNTERS IN THE NEW TESTAMENT THAT JESUS HAD WITH JOHN:

1. MARK 9:38-41

John was not perfect; he grew in his knowledge and understanding. We see Jesus reproving him and instructing him in this text. Jesus told him not to rebuke someone who was casting out demons even though they did not belong to their small group. John later recorded Jesus' words in John 10:16, "And other sheep I have which are not of this fold; them also I must bring, and they will hear My voice; and there will be one flock and one shepherd."

2. LUKE 9:51-56

Here we see why Jesus called them the sons of thunder in Mark 3:17! The two brothers could be volatile and given to a temper. It is good to remember that John was a man who grew in his relationship with Christ through trials, failures, and setbacks just like you and me.

Jesus literally rebuked these two brothers James and John and He did so firmly. At times we can become very judgmental and overly harsh toward people. But not Christ. He was holy but loving. There is no perfect human being and no perfect church. With Jesus, school was always in session with the disciples. He was creating men to whom He could turn over His ministry. We really need to follow Christ and seek to build people and make disciples instead of just trying to win them to Christ. It is both/and.

3. MARK 10:35-45

James and John asked Christ if they could sit at His right hand and His left hand in heaven. I think it reveals, among other things, their faith in Jesus; they knew who He was and that He would reign in glory.

But notice the way Jesus answers them, and how He teaches them and us a valuable lesson about greatness. Morgan writes, "That day He revealed to John that the way to the position of power in His kingdom was the way of the cross, of the passion baptism of suffering and of sacrifice. They had a good way to travel before they arrived, but what is noticeable is that He did not sharply rebuke them but revealed to them the secrets of the power they sought."[73]

Dr. Al Fasol, my preaching professor at Southwestern, said the high-water text in the New Testament is Mark 10:45, and what an awesome verse it is!

4. JOHN 19:26-27

Jesus entrusts John with the care of Mary; this is a revealing word because it shows us the trust and confidence Jesus had in John. Tradition says that he cared for Mary until her death.

LESSONS FROM JOHN'S LIFE

1. EVEN THE GREATEST OF JESUS' DISCIPLES HAVE TO GROW IN GRACE.

As we have seen with Peter, we see with John. He was not perfect, but Jesus shaped and molded him. **Jesus saved John in a moment but sanctified him for the remainder of his life.**

That is true of us as well. This should make us more patient with others and ourselves. "He's still working on me, to make me what I ought to be."

It is good to keep in mind that even the greatest of men and women are still men and women and they must not be placed on a pedestal.

Would you care to guess who is quoted as saying, "I am not, or ever have been, in favor of bringing about in any way the social and political equality of the white and black races. I am not or ever have been in favor of making voters or jurors of Negroes, nor of qualifying them to hold office." Abraham Lincoln made these comments in 1858. [74]

Even the greatest of our presidents of the USA, Abraham Lincoln, was still a mortal man and sinned and fell short like us all. I appreciate that about David Herbert Donald's biography of Lincoln, that he brings out the president's weaknesses as well as strengths.

2. JESUS CALLS MEN FROM *THEIR* PROFESSION TO *HIS*.

Jesus takes our natural abilities and uses those abilities for the furtherance of the Gospel. John was an intelligent man, a thinker, a mystic, and a man of great intellectual abilities. God took those natural endowments that He had given John and used them for the ministry.

God does not call everyone into vocational ministry. But He certainly calls some. If God has not called you to vocational service, then please know He still has called you to serve Him in His church and He desires for you to serve Him by using the abilities He has given you.

Some are great speakers and teachers and need to teach. Some are gifted servants and need to serve. Some are great with their hands and can build things and fix things. There are men in our church who have these gifts and use them in helping widows and others who are in need. You are to use the gifts God has given you to help people in the church and on mission trips.

3. TO FINISH THE CHRISTIAN LIFE WELL IS THE GREATEST SERVICE RENDERED TO JESUS CHRIST.

John shows us how to finish well. He is well into his nineties when he dies. Toward the end of his life, even after serving as one of the original twelve apostles, serving as the pastor of the church at Ephesus, writing the Gospel of John and the three Epistles of John, he writes the book of Revelation while exiled on the island of Patmos.

I heard a pastor say, "The devil does not mind waiting on you." That is a sobering thought when you think about it. The devil is determined to destroy our Christian witness and testimony for Christ and he will wait while we are strong and attack us when we are weak or vulnerable. He seeks to bring us to ruin and to hurt the cause of Christ. I do not know of anything that brings more shame to Christ and damage to the Christian faith than when pastors or active church members fall into some egregious sin.

The older I become, the more determined I am to not only start well and serve well, but most of all finish well.

John became one of God's trophies of grace. God saved this fisherman with a great mind and short temper, and then called him into the ministry and used him powerfully for the kingdom of God.

CHAPTER 8

THE APOSTLE PHILLIP

The next day Jesus decided to leave for Galilee.
He found Philip and told him, "Follow me."
Now Philip was from Bethsaida,
the hometown of Andrew and Peter.
Philip found Nathanael and told him,
"We have found the one Moses wrote about in the law
(and so did the prophets):
Jesus the son of Joseph, from Nazareth."
"Can anything good come out of Nazareth?"
Nathanael asked him.
"Come and see," Philip answered.

—JOHN 1:43-46

Look at another of the twelve original Apostles of Jesus Christ, a man named Philip. The name Philip means "lover of horses." Matthew, Mark, and Luke only list that he was an apostle. Everything we learn about Philip, we learn from the Gospel of John. He is mentioned four times by John.

Philip did not seek after Christ, as Andrew and John did.

John says Jesus found him (John 1:43). Perhaps he did not have the same religious drive or spiritual sensitivities as the others, but the Lord found him and used him.

John Foxe, in his book *Voices of the Martyrs*, writes this of Philip, "Philip's Greek name, his multilingual abilities, and his outgoing personality all combined with his vibrant faith in the risen Christ to make him an equipped messenger for the gospel." Philip took the Gospel to what we know today as France (Gaul back then). According to tradition, he also evangelized western Turkey, to Hierapolis, where he was stoned and crucified. [75]

FOUR ENCOUNTERS CHRIST HAD WITH PHILIP

1. JOHN 1:43-46

"The next day Jesus decided to leave for Galilee. He found Philip and told him, 'Follow me.' Now Philip was from Bethsaida, the hometown of Andrew and Peter. Philip found Nathanael and told him, 'We have found the one Moses wrote about in the law (and so did the prophets): Jesus the son of Joseph, from Nazareth.' 'Can anything good come out of Nazareth?' Nathanael asked him. 'Come and see,' Philip answered."

G. Campbell Morgan refers to Philip as being an unimpressive man. He told Nathanael to come and see and did not give an argument or explanation. Perhaps he did not have the intellectual acumen of others, but he must be recognized for his prompt faith and obedience when he responded to Jesus' call to follow Him. And he should be commended for his witnessing to Nathanael. I think it is a wise thing to tell someone who is skeptical or doubting Jesus to search Him out and look for yourself. Or encourage someone who has questions to read the Bible. Start with the Gospel of John.

D.A. Carson writes about verse 45, "As Andrew brought Simon Peter and perhaps Philip to Jesus, so *Philip found Nathanael* and witnessed to him. That has been the foundational principle of truly Christian expansion ever since: new followers of Jesus bear witness of him to others, who in turn become disciples and repeat the process."[76]

2. JOHN 6:5-7

"So when Jesus looked up and noticed a huge crowd coming toward him, he asked Philip, 'Where will we buy bread so that these people can eat?' He asked this to test him, for he himself knew what he was going to do. Philip answered him, 'Two hundred denarii worth of bread wouldn't be enough for each of them to have a little."

Jesus questions people throughout the Scriptures. Here He questions Philip as a test of his faith. And Philip responded like many of us would. He looks at the *impossible* instead of looking at the *God of the impossible*.

Dr. Fish says, "Jesus was drawing Philip out into commitment. Jesus was trying to get Philip to see that one piece of bread PLUS JESUS was enough. He wanted Philip to see His adequacy."

Carson writes, "In this instance Philip was the obvious person to ask: he came from the nearby town of Bethsaida (John 1:44). Specification of such details may therefore more reasonably be taken as evidence for the recollection of an eyewitness.

"In John 6:6, John adds this comment to forestall any reader from thinking that Jesus was stumped or surprised by the miracle that was eventually performed. The Evangelist avers that Jesus already had his own plan, but that the problem itself gave him a further opportunity to test Philip. The verb *peirazø* ('test') is commonly used by the Evangelist in the bad sense of 'tempt', to solicit to do evil. The word itself, however, is neutral, and is entirely appropriate here.

"In John 6:7, Philip's response betrays the fact that he can think only at the level of the marketplace, the natural world. One *denarius* was a day's pay for a common laborer; two hundred *denarii* (also specifically stated in Mark 6:37) therefore represents *eight months' wages.* Since a substantial proportion of a worker's wage went into daily food, this was, presumably, enough to provide for a family for eight months or a little longer. But the crowd was so large (John 6:10) that even such a large sum of money *would not buy enough bread for each one to have a bite!"* [77]

I can relate to Philip here, as often when the Lord tests me I fail, because I do not trust Him. It is so easy to see the human, the limitations, the lack, but God wants us to see Him, and when we see Him we are satisfied and blessed.

3. JOHN 12:20-26

"Now some Greeks were among those who went up to worship at the festival. So they came to Philip, who was from Bethsaida in Galilee, and requested of him, 'Sir, we want to see Jesus.' Philip went and told Andrew; then Andrew and Philip went and told Jesus.

Jesus replied to them, 'The hour has come for the Son of Man to be glorified. Truly I tell you, unless a grain of wheat falls to the ground and dies, it remains by itself. But if it dies, it produces much fruit. The one who loves his life will lose it, and the one who hates his life in this world will keep it for eternal life. If anyone serves me, he must follow me. Where I am, there my servant also will be. If anyone serves me, the Father will honor him."

Morgan sees indecisiveness in Philip, which is a reason why he will refer to him as unimpressive. [78] Perhaps Morgan is a bit harsh on Philip. Philip does not know exactly what to do so he goes to get help from Andrew. "To see" means to *interview*.

Perhaps Jesus' popularity had reached their ears (Carson believes it could stem from them hearing about Jesus overturning the table in the Temple of those who sold animals.) However, Jesus did not come to be interviewed and made popular; He came for the express purpose of dying for the sins of the world, Jew and Gentile alike.

I love John 12:24. It is simple and yet extremely profound. In Fyodor Dostoevsky's *The Brother's Karamazov*, he lists a passage of Scripture at the front of his book. It is ironic because some believe it presents great challenges to the Christian faith.

I read the book a few years ago and it is indeed fascinating. The reason it is purported to present such a challenge to Christianity is because it focuses on the problem of evil and suffering. But the one biblical passage listed at the front of the book is John 12:24, "Truly I tell you, unless a grain of wheat falls to the ground and dies, it remains by itself. But if it dies, it produces much fruit." The author begins his book with this verse because he knows it is true.

I personally think Philip is impressive at this point. He and Andrew attempt to introduce these Greeks to the Lord. And this gave occasion to a profound word from Jesus about salvation, not just for a few Greeks, but also for the whole world. Jesus was going to the cross to die and in so dying He would change many, just as the grain that dies in the ground produces a large harvest. What an unforgettable lesson for the disciples and for us. We too must die to self. In so doing God brings about a great harvest through us.

4. JOHN 14:7-11

"If you know me, you will also know my Father. From now on you do know him and have seen him."
"Lord," said Philip, "show us the Father, and that's enough for us."
Jesus said to him, 'Have I been among you all this time and you do not know me, Philip? The one who has seen me has seen the Father. How can you say, 'Show us the Father'? Don't you believe that I am in the Father and the Father is in me? The words I speak to you I do not speak on my own. The Father who lives in me does his works. Believe me that I am in the Father and the Father is in me. Otherwise, believe because of the works themselves"

Jesus questions and then rebukes Philip for his lack of understanding. Philip verbalized perhaps what the others were thinking. He did not understand, so he asks the question, and his very question revealed just how much he did not understand. Jesus calls him out by name and yes, rebukes him, but also teaches him and the others some valuable spiritual insight into the very nature of who Jesus is.

Jesus and the Father are one, and when Philip and the others look upon Jesus Christ they are looking upon the express image of God the Father. Colossians 1:15 states, "He [Jesus] is the image of the invisible God, the firstborn over all creation."

The Lord takes an encounter with Philip to reveal truths that we are, even today, 2,000 years later, reading and appreciating.

Carson comments, "The Evangelist has already made it clear in his Prologue that however mitigated God's gracious self-disclosure was in former times, in Jesus he has made himself known, definitively, gloriously, visibly (cf. notes on 1:14, 18; cf. 12:45)."[79]

LESSONS LEARNED FROM PHILIP

What are some lessons that we can learn from the life of Philip and how the Lord dealt with him?

1. GOD CALLS ALL TYPES OF PEOPLE TO FOLLOW HIM.

Philip may not have been a thinker or even as intelligent as say the Apostle John. In fact, Morgan would say he was not very intelligent and he therefore calls him "unimpressive." Philip may have been slower to understand than others, but the Lord loved him and chose him to be one of His apostles.

When Jesus chose Philip to follow Him it reveals to us today that He uses all types, all personalities, the brilliant and not so brilliant. He uses people like John, Martin Luther, John Calvin, Jonathan Edwards, C.S. Lewis and other geniuses, and He also chooses and uses ordinary people like Philip and me.

The Lord calls everyone to follow Him. And all of us have different gifts and talents that we use in service to our Lord. It is useless to spend time focusing on what gifts we lack or how some are more blessed in some areas than others. We must trust God and capitalize on what gifts and abilities we do possess and use them for service to our King.

Being content in who you are or comfortable in your own skin is very liberating. God is sovereign, and He chooses the gifts we have. We must be at peace with this and serve God with all we have and not try and compare ourselves to others. Comparison is the devil's doings and brings only conflict and no peace.

2. JESUS IS ENOUGH.

Jesus is enough. Philip was looking at the scenario strictly from a human viewpoint. He looked only at the empirical, relying on what was before him. He calculated that it would take 200 denarii to feed so many people. There were 5,000 men alone. But when you look upon Jesus you see God in the flesh. Jesus is all we need.

We are all faced with what looks to us to be insurmountable odds or obstacles. But with Jesus with us and in us, and His Holy Spirit empowering us, we are going to win! God will accomplish all He desires. Our role is to trust Him and walk in His power.

3. God still tests His children.

In John 6:6, Jesus clearly tests Philip. Jesus knew all along what He would do. Is God testing you today? Are you faced with what seems to be an impossible situation like it was for Philip?

The correct way to respond is something like this: "I don't know what to do God, but I know you know, so instead of me worrying and trying to figure it out, I will trust in You, and wait on you to tell me what to do."

4. Introduce others to Jesus.

Jesus called Philip, and then Philip goes and evangelizes Nathaniel. There are people to whom God will lead you. You will need to be sensitive to the Holy Spirit as He leads you in sharing your faith with them. You will be much more effective in reaching some people than I will be. The key to the expansion of the kingdom of God here on earth is every believer sharing Jesus, or every beggar telling other beggars where to find bread.

Great Hills Baptist Church held an ordination service for our son, Bryant, Afterwards, we went to Outback Steakhouse for dinner. There was a couple in the parking lot who were in the process of moving from Los Angeles to Austin. Their truck had been broken into and everything they had was stolen—phone, purse, keyboards, etc. Their names were Tom and Linda. She was crying and having a really hard time. They were in the city to meet with a realtor to find a place to live.

When I gave her my card and offered to pray with her she said, "We are born-again Christians!" We stayed with them about 30 minutes, and all the folks with us pitched in and gave them over $300. They were so appreciative. If they move somewhere in this vicinity, I do believe they will come to Great Hills. They were our "ones."

Blair Eddins and Brian Tilley are good friends of mine that I met while I served as their interim pastor twenty-two years ago. They are fine men of God, growing in the Lord and serving Him. They both told me about the man whom God used to bring them to Jesus. His name was Wally Teasener.

Wally was bold and aggressive in his evangelistic tactics. He would challenge Blair and Brian to give their lives to the Lord. Blair told me that it took someone like Wally to reach him because he would walk around or walk through someone if they were not as bold. Brian, who is such a funny guy, told me how he would sit in his house with a pair of shorts on with no shirt, long hair, tattoos, living a life indulgent in alcohol and drugs. Wally just kept coming after him. Wally first got Brian's name from the visitor's card that he filled out at church when he came to see his dad get baptized. Wally had led his dad to the Lord.

One particular night Brian said he saw Wally coming up to his house and he thought, "Oh my, what is he doing here again?" But that night Wally led Brian to Christ. Now Brian leads mission teams from Green Pines Baptist Church in North Carolina to Bangladesh! And Blair is involved in missions and using his resources to bless many ministries that are reaching people with the Gospel.

5. WHO IS YOUR "ONE" THIS WEEK?

Robert Coleman says in his *Master Plan of Evangelism* that sharing Christ is not an important element of our lives but the important core purpose of our lives.

God loves to answer this prayer: Lead me Lord to someone who needs You and grant me the wisdom and the boldness to tell them about You.

FOR
THE
ONE

CHAPTER 9

NATHANIEL

Then Jesus saw Nathanael coming toward him and said about him,
"Here truly is an Israelite in whom there is no deceit."
How do you know me?" Nathanael asked.
"Before Philip called you, when you were under the fig tree, I saw you,"
Jesus answered.
"Rabbi," Nathanael replied, "You are the Son of God;
you are the King of Israel!"
Jesus responded to him, "Do you believe because I told you
I saw you under the fig tree?
You will see greater things than this."
Then he said, "Truly I tell you, you will see heaven opened
and the angels of God ascending and descending on the Son of Man."

—JOHN 1:47-51

While it is certainly a good thing to have time alone, God has called us to people; and we cannot become hermits and monks or adopt a monastic lifestyle. Jesus loves people and so do His followers. He left the ninety-nine to pursue the one lost sheep. I am so very glad He left heaven to come to earth to show the way for me to have forgiveness and eternal life!

John 1:43-51 focuses on Jesus witnessing to and ministering to a man named Nathanael, whose name means "gift of God." He most likely is also the same man referred to as Bartholomew, one of Jesus' original twelve Apostles.

Nathanael is mentioned in John 21:2 with some other disciples at the Sea of Galilee and also in Acts 1:13 in the Upper Room. It is good to read that Nathanael starts well and finishes well with the Lord, unlike another apostle, Judas.

Regarding Nathanael or Bartholomew, John Foxe, states, "Traditions have him traveling east, as far as regions called India, but the historical consensus locates his ministry and martyrdom in Armenia—a land to the northeast of Palestine, between the Black and Caspian Seas." [80]

Many were led to Christ and baptized, and the local religious leaders brought swift persecution. Nathanael was flayed where his skin was removed from his body in a gruesome form of torture and then crucified upside down. The many biblical sites marked by shrines and churches that were built by Armenian Christians are signs of the effectiveness of Nathanael's ministry. [81]

May God help each one of us finish the Christian life well. One of my mottos in life is "no regret." I hope to live my life with passion and fervor for Christ, so that those who come after me can be encouraged to live for Christ. I hope to live in such a way that you can put these words on my tombstone: "NO REGRETS." I do not want to look back on my life with a lot of statements that begin with "I wish I had..."

What can we learn about this man named Nathanael? What can we learn from Jesus in the way that He deals with Nathanael that will help us as we reach the ones God places before us to reach?

Let us look at Nathanael from these four perspectives: *evangelized, evasive, engaged, and equipped.*

EVANGELIZED (JOHN 1:45-46)

Nathanael lived in Cana, a town about nine miles due north from Nazareth, the distance from the University of Texas to Great Hills Baptist Church. I think he was an intelligent, searching, seeking soul. I believe he was an intellectual who was a little opinionated. But he was open to divine truth, and fortunately for him Philip was not intimidated by him and reached out to him.

Verse 45 says Philip found Nathanael. Philip impresses me with his evangelistic zeal to reach out to his friend. Philip is intentional in his evangelism. He did not wait for Nathanael to ask him; rather, Philip took the initiative and spoke to him.

Dr. Ed Stetzer encourages Christ-followers to be intentional and simply talk to people that we already know. They are a lot more open to spiritual matters than we think. He writes, "Moreover, the survey showed that almost 90% of unchurched Americans say they have at least one close friend who considers himself or herself a Christian. Do those Christians talk too much about their beliefs? Not according to seventy-one of survey respondents. Despite their bad attitudes toward the church, unchurched Americans are surprisingly open to talking about the Christian faith and, in fact, already know someone who could talk to them about Jesus…All we need to do is start conversations about spiritual matters with the unchurched people we already know. They're waiting."[82]

Notice that in John 1:45, Philip says, "We have found Him." I think Philip has joy and enthusiasm as he speaks to his friend about Jesus. He is excited about the wonderful discovery, and he wants Nathanael to know Jesus as well.

Philip says, "We have found Him whom Moses wrote about." Here are some Biblical texts that speak of the Messiah in the Pentateuch: Genesis 3:15, 12:3; and Deuteronomy 18:15, 18. Also Philip says that the prophets wrote about Jesus as well. There are hundreds of references we could cite, but here are a few of my favorites:

"Therefore, the Lord himself will give you a sign: See, the virgin will conceive, have a son, and name him Immanuel."

—ISAIAH 7:14

"For a child will be born for us, a son will be given to us, and the government will be on his shoulders. He will be named Wonderful Counselor, Mighty God, Eternal Father, Prince of Peace."

—ISAIAH 9:6

"Bethlehem Ephrathah, you are small among clans of Judah; one will come from you to be ruler over Israel for me. His origin is antiquity, from ancient times."

—MICAH 5:2

"The Lord your God will raise up for you a prophet like me from among your own brothers. You must listen to him."

—DEUTERONOMY 18:15

Philip also tells him specifically who this individual is and where He is from. The name Jesus means Savior. The equivalent name in the Old Testament is Joshua, a fact that I believe Nathanael knew quite well. Then Philip tells Nathanael where He is from—Jesus of Nazareth.

Nazareth is the town where Jesus was raised by Joseph and Mary. Not Rome, Athens, Antioch, Alexandria, or Corinth, or Ephesus or a host of other major cities; no, He is from Nazareth. While visiting the Holy Land, we stopped and overlooked the city of Nazareth; it is a small town today, just as it was in Jesus' day.

I love Philip's response to Nathanael's rather jaded, evasive answer—he tells him, "Come and see." Come see for yourself, Mr. Nathanael. That very much appealed to Nathanael, and in verse 47, we read where he comes to Jesus.

EVASIVE (JOHN 1:46-47)

Notice in verse 46, how Nathanael responds to the invitation of Philip by stating, "Can anything good come out of Nazareth?" His initial response to Philip's witnessing to him was one of brushing him off, so to speak. It is the same way many times today. **Lost people just try to brush us away, but if we respond with kindness and tactfulness, we will often see that their initial no is really a hesitant yes.**

I read an interesting book entitled *Never Split the Difference*, by Chris Voss, a former high-level hostage negotiator. The book is a secular one with little reference to spiritual matters. However, I learned a lot about how to deal with people while reading this book. Voss has some jewels of knowledge that will help you in any negotiation, since all truth is God's truth.

Voss espouses basic principles like listen well, be humble, seek to understand and then seek to make sure you are understood, and look for the Black Swans in conversations. It's an interesting idea, as there are not many of these, but they do exist, and in a negotiation you have to look for them. Black swans are pieces of information that you have to look and listen for because they can turn the conversation in a very favorable way. The Black Swan for Nathanael was when Jesus told him "I saw you." He had no idea Jesus had this kind of supernatural knowledge.

Nathanael actually spoke the truth and was straightforward because Nazareth had the reputation, and rightfully so, of being a town of corruption. It was located on a hillside. At the bottom of the hill there was a highway that the Roman soldiers, as well as merchants or businessmen, would travel. They would stop there at night. Morgan says, "It was rotten to the core." [83] Nathanael knew his Old Testament and it said nothing of Nazareth. John MacArthur believes because the two towns were so close together, about ten miles, that there was maybe some hostility or rivalry between Nathanael's hometown of Cana and Jesus' hometown of Nazareth. [84]

Philip just tells him to come and see, which I think is an excellent response to the intellectual. See for yourself. Nathanael took Philip up on the offer, as we read in verse 47. Philip gives us great instruction and encouragement by his actions.

When sharing Christ with someone, we are not responsible for his or her conversion; we are only responsible to tell them. They have to decide for themselves. But let us always do our part and at least care for and speak to them.

When you talk to your one this week, or your two or three, and you sense push-back, you can do what Philip did, and just say, "Come see for yourself." I heard about one of our church members witnessing to an atheist. He told him, "Read the Bible for a year for an hour every day and then let us talk. You can't summarily dismiss something you don't at least understand." Invite them to read the Gospel of John, or attend church with you and hear the pastor speak.

ENGAGED (JOHN 1:47-49)

Notice the way Jesus speaks to Nathanael is verse 47; He gives him a word of compliment. He calls him an "Israelite indeed, in whom is no deceit." The Greek word is *dolos*, and it means decoy, trick, craft, and deceit. When encountering people it is always good to remember the power of a positive word, a word of blessing and compliment. A stroke of blessing is much better than a poke of criticism. Also, honey attracts much better than vinegar.

I met a couple of college graduates from Boston, now living in Austin. One was a chemical engineer and the other a data specialist, and one of the first things I said was something like, "That is great, you guys are very intelligent." I spoke to them about who we are as a church and how we love people and invited them to visit with us.

Morgan points out that he sees two references to the Old Testament patriarch Jacob in this text. First, notice the word deceit or guile. Jacob's name means supplanter, deceitful, literally one who takes the heel, and he was known for his deceit. But God changed his name to Israel in Genesis 32:28. The name Israel means "prince with God." The second reference to Jacob that Morgan sees is in verse 51, which we will look at later.

In verse 48, we see that Nathanael is impressed and asked how Jesus knows him, as they had never met. The Lord told him he had seen him under the fig tree. That is impressive, as no one was around when he was under the tree.

Dr. Roy Fish says, "Something significant happened under a fig tree. It was probably Nathanael's favorite place of prayer. It was here that he got alone with the God of Abraham, where he met the Lord. In all likelihood, recently he had been under this fig tree with a desperate hunger in his heart to know more about the Messiah. Jesus knew the thoughts of Nathanael as he communed with God there. 'The thing you hungered for there under the fig tree I saw—and the answer to your hunger is here.' Nathanael confesses Christ."

Jesus' words, "I saw you," are so simple and yet powerful. The Lord sees us when we think He does not see us. He watches over us, He cares for us, and He desires us to know Him. Jesus saw him. May God help us see others this week with the eyes of Jesus. Some time ago, while in Orlando for a pastors golf retreat, I was sitting at a restaurant next to David Uth, pastor of First Baptist Church, Orlando, Florida, as he was talking about the power of touch, just reaching out and physically touching someone.

About that time this man came up to him and you could tell he was upset. He had come into the restaurant and seen the group of pastors and asked, "Who are these guys?"

He was told they are a group of pastors, and the guy prayed, "Lord, I need a sign from you to show me you care for me; please let Pastor David be one of those pastors."

It was amazing to watch David look the man in the eye, touch him, listen to him and then pray for him. So many people are searching for a sign from God. If we will slow down and see people, God can use us greatly, and we can be the answer to their prayers.

Jesus has Nathanael's full and undivided attention. Nathanael is deeply engaged in this evangelistic encounter with Jesus Christ. He responds correctly to who Jesus is and affirms his belief in Christ, and I believe at this moment the somewhat cynical Nathanael is saved, born again.

Have you ever made that confession of faith to Jesus expressing your personal faith and trust in Him? Nathanael did and he meant it, and you know how we know he was for real? We see him staying with the Lord and the disciples in John 21:2 and again in Acts 1:13 in the Upper Room before Pentecost, praying with the other believers.

EQUIPPED (JOHN 1:50-51)

I sense the Lord gently rebuking Nathanael as He equips and disciples him. Jesus told him he would see greater things than these, and indeed Nathanael did as He followed the Lord for three and a half years. Think of all the amazing things he saw, the miracles of our Lord recorded for us in the Gospels—raising the dead, healing the crippled, the blind and the lepers, feeding the multitudes, and all the other amazing things that Jesus did.

This is a promise not only for Nathanael but also for all who follow the Lord as well. When we step out in faith and see the Lord initially in salvation this is only the beginning, because the Lord will allow us to see Him work in wonderful ways as we walk with Him.

Look at John 1:51. Jacob had the vision where he saw the angels ascending and descending in Genesis 28:12. In *The Holy Bible—Baptist Study Edition* are these interpretive words, "Jacob's dream assured him that in spite of his deceit the blessings of the Abrahamic covenant would pass through him . . . . Hence the Lord is called the God of Abraham, Isaac, and Jacob (Exodus 3:15). The ladder, a symbol of blessing from heaven, is interpreted by Jesus as a type of Himself, the One fulfilling the covenant (John 1:51)."[85]

My favorite quote in Morgan's chapter on Nathanael is the one where he describes the encounter that Jacob had with the Angel of the Lord, where He wrestled with the Angel of the Lord in Genesis 32. (A Christophany is what some scholars call this; Morgan writes about Jacob, "Thus God had crippled him to crown him, had broken him to make him, had mastered him to give him majesty."[86]

What a powerful truth this is. Perhaps Jesus is dealing with Nathanael in a way that is similar to the way He dealt with the patriarch Jacob. A blessing in verse 51 follows the rebuke in verse 50.

One writer states, regarding our text in verse 51, "Being under the fig tree possibly signified study of the Old Testament. Perhaps Nathanael had been meditating on the account of Jacob's ladder vision (Genesis 28:12). Jesus tells the disciples they will see a much greater sight: the Son of Man's glory in His ministry among them. Jesus replaces any mediating link with heaven, for He is the unique 'Bethel,' God's dwelling with men (Genesis 28:17; John 1:14)." [87]

MacArthur says the significance of this statement in verse 51 is that Jesus is the mediator between God and man. [88]

The last thing I want to point out in our text is the way Jesus refers to Himself in verse 51. Nathanael had rightly referred to Jesus as the Son of God, and Jesus here uses the phrase Son of Man. This was Jesus' favorite title for Himself. It is used thirteen times in John's Gospel and almost eighty times in all the Gospels. [89] Jesus is fully God and fully man. As a man He related to us in our humanity and as God, He offers us eternal forgiveness and pardon of sin.

You have to love the way the Lord deals with people in the New Testament. He never deals with any two people in the same way. **Jesus knows who they are and arranges His encounter so that it has the maximum effect.** May we follow our Lord's example and get out among the people, find our "ones," and love them, share with them, and point them to the Christ even as Philip did.

Remember—people want to talk about Jesus; yes, some of your friends would be open if you were to have a conversation about Christ. Unfortunately, there are more people who want to hear about the Lord than there are those who are willing to tell them.

FOR
THE
ONE

CHAPTER 10

MATTHEW

As Jesus went on from there,
he saw a man named Matthew sitting at the toll booth,
and he said to him, "Follow me,"
and he got up and followed him.
While he was reclining at the table in the house,
many tax collectors and sinners came
to eat with Jesus and his disciples.
When the Pharisees saw this, they asked his disciples,
"Why does your teacher eat with tax collectors and sinners?"
Now when he heard this, he said,
"It is not those who are well who need a doctor,
but those who are sick. Go and learn what this means:
I desire mercy and not sacrifice.
For I didn't come to call the righteous, but sinners."

—MATTHEW 9:9-13

All three Synoptic Gospels record the calling of Matthew also known as Levi. Jesus told Matthew to follow Him, and Matthew did just that. We have no record of Matthew saying anything; he simply obeyed Jesus and followed Him, became His disciple. Jesus did not tell Matthew to follow Him and He will make him to be a fisher of men as he did to Peter and Andrew (Matthew 4:19-20). Matthew was not a fisherman by trade.

Matthew's name can mean *gift from God* or it can mean *faithful*. [90] Matthew never calls himself by the name Levi; he always refers to himself as Matthew. Mark and Luke call him Levi and then later list him by the name Matthew. Morgan believes Jesus changed his name from Levi to Matthew.

In John Foxe's *Voices of the Martyrs*, he writes, "Given Matthew's passion to reach Israelites with the good news about their Messiah, we shouldn't be surprised to discover various traditions about Matthew's ministry among the widely scattered communities of Jews throughout the Roman Empire. As an itinerant missionary, it's quite possible that Matthew visited many locations. Matthew's apostolic assignment was to Ethiopia. . . . Traditional consensus has leaned toward placing Matthew in African Ethiopia, where he was beheaded while carrying out Jesus' commission to reach the world." [91]

Morgan says we know three things about Matthew:

1. HE WAS A HEBREW.

He was a narrow man like the other Hebrews who were proud of their history. Morgan writes, and I thought this was interesting, especially since it was written in 1937, "That, [the fact that Matthew was narrow] in certain ways, is an excellent quality. We are cursed today with a passion of breadth. A little more narrowness would strengthen the whole host of the people of God." [92]

I agree; there are times to be narrow, especially in theology— there is one God, not many; there is one way to heaven through Christ; there are morals and laws to follow, etc.

2. HE WAS A PUBLICAN OR TAX COLLECTOR.

He was a Jew, but he was employed by Herod and the Romans. He, like Zacchaeus, was not well-liked by his fellow countrymen. Matthew and Zacchaeus were looked upon as traitors to their country. The Talmud placed them in the same category as thieves and murderers. The Roman historian, Tacitus, says there was a statue built for one honest tax collector because there were so few of them!

Tax collectors or publicans were sharp men in finance and accounting. But they were disliked by their fellow Jews because (1) they worked for the Romans and (2) they would charge more than the fixed tariff or tax, thereby becoming wealthy at the Jews' expense. [93]

3. HE WAS PROFOUNDLY RELIGIOUS.

Before knowing Jesus, Morgan says, Matthew had a thorough knowledge of the Old Testament. In the Gospel that bears his name, Matthew quotes more from the Old Testament than all the other Gospel writers combined. He makes ninety-nine direct references to Old Testament passages of Scripture. He uses a phrase that Mark, Luke, and John do not use, "That it might be fulfilled."

Morgan writes, "Thus, though he may have been looked upon by his contemporaries as a renegade, he was no renegade from the Hebrew religion. He had studied their writings in a remarkable way, and we may safely deduce the fact that he was a profoundly religious man." [94]

THE COMMAND (MATTHEW 9:9)

In Matthew 9:9, Jesus meets Matthew in or outside Capernaum, a city on the northwest section of the Sea of Galilee, a city that Christ made as the base of His operations for His ministry at this time. [95]

Dr. Fish says that Jesus spent at least a year and a half living in the city of Capernaum. Matthew would collect his taxes or tariffs from the fishermen as they brought in their catch or from merchants traveling across the sea with their goods. [96] Dr. Fish points out that there was a road that traveled from Babylon to Rome and it passed through Capernaum. Goods brought in from foreign countries would be taxed. The purpose of the Roman taxes was primarily used for three things: roads, soldiers, and public buildings.

Matthew was sitting at his excise or customs booth when Christ passed by and spoke to him the words, "Follow me" in Matthew 9:9. This is different than when Jesus says "Follow me" in Matthew 4:19, which is *deute opiso*. The word used in Matthew 9:9 is the word *akoloutheo*, present active imperative; it means to be in the same way with, to accompany, to follow. *Akoloutheo* is also used in Matthew 16:24. [97]

Matthew probably had heard of Christ. Perhaps he had heard Him teaching others and was ready to follow. I wonder what had been going on in Matthew's life; we do not know, but the Bible says he arose and followed Jesus.

D.A. Carson mentions that some scholars believe that it is quite unlikely that a man on the outskirts of Jewish life could be the author of the Gospel of Matthew, but Carson replies, "But does it not also seem unlikely that "a son of thunder" should become the apostle of love, or that the arch-persecutor of the church should become its greatest missionary and theologian?" [98]

I agree, we can never underestimate the power of Jesus to save and change a life!

THE MEETING (MATTHEW 9:10)

Mark and Luke specify that it was in Matthew's house (Matthew 9:10) where Jesus met with many tax collectors and sinners. Sinners could mean those who did not obey all the points of the law of the Pharisees and it also could include people like harlots, tax collectors, and others regarded as outcasts.

Dr. Fish writes these words regarding Matthew bringing others to hear Jesus: "Matthew's reaction is a thrilling thing. I think he understood Jesus best of all. He knew what pleased Him the most—to preach to more people like himself. No sooner was he converted than he arranged a party and called the publicans and the harlots and the sinners. This reflects the kind of company Matthew had been forced into. Jesus had the privilege of preaching to them. The Bible says there were many, and they followed Him. When Matthew was reached by Jesus, immediately he wanted to reach others of his class."

Take note again of where they are meeting—in Matthew's house. New believers have many lost family members and friends, and we as church leaders need to seize these moments of spreading the gospel through those family and friend ties that the new believer already has. Matthew was a new Christian and he invited Jesus to his house. He also invited his buddies, people like him who needed the Savior. Note that Jesus accepted the invitation from Matthew and He went to where the sinners were.

Carson says, "There is no suggestion here that He went to sinners because they gladly received Him; rather, He went to them because they were sinners, just as a doctor goes to the sick because they are sick." [99]

THE QUESTION (MATTHEW 9:11)

In verse 11, the Pharisees asked Jesus' disciples their question in an accusatory fashion, not in a genuine desire to obtain information. There is sarcasm in their voice when they make their request.

For the Pharisees, it was unthinkable to eat with those whom they classified as sinners, those who did not keep all the stringent requirements of the law that they took pride in keeping.

Jesus was way outside their comfort zone. Instead of listening and learning, they would rather accuse and condemn. That is always the temptation for those of us who are religious—we accuse and condemn something we do not like or that we do not understand, which is tragic. God help us never to become Pharisees.

I have seen this same scenario play out frequently in church. When you do something new or different in order to reach people, do not expect everyone to rejoice, join in and offer to help. Oftentimes the desire to reach lost souls headed to hell is not enough motivation to appease those who prefer church to be exactly what they like.

It is not just here in the USA. I have a missionary friend named Jeff. He has quite the testimony of how God used him and his family on an island in the Indian Ocean. I call him the LeBron James of missionaries. When he went there to serve, they only baptized four to five people a year. He said, "This is unacceptable," and he changed things up and went after lost people. They baptized around 1,000 people and planted numerous churches. Jeff said those who criticized him the most were the Christians.

THE ANSWER (MATTHEW 9:12-13)

Look at Jesus' response. Again, He uses an analogy to make His point. He tells them that the well do not need a doctor, but the sick need help. Those who are sinners are indeed sick and in need of care.

This was a stinging word of confrontation to the religious leaders. They knew that these people were sinners and away from God and they should have been the ones loving and ministering to them.

We must always be careful in the church that we do not become like the Pharisees in Jesus' day. It is so easy to become self-righteous and judgmental and forget the very reason God saved us in the first place, which is to love lost people and help them.

People in the church will gravitate toward fighting and not fishing. A friend of mine was getting ready to go visit some people on a Wednesday night, when a church member confronted him and wanted to argue a point and be contentious. My friend, who is an associate pastor at the church, told the person, "Excuse me, I do not have time to talk about this because I am going out on visitation to tell someone about Jesus."

The Pharisees were extremely concerned about ceremonial defilement caused from eating with such lowlife, but that did not deter Jesus and His disciples as they ate with and shared with the sinners in Matthew's house.

Jesus told the religious scholars to go and learn in Matthew 9:13. "Go and learn what this means" is a rabbinic formula meaning that they needed to go and study further. Surely this did not sit well with the learned Pharisees when this person, who was defiled in their estimation, was telling them they needed to go and study some more!

Jesus quotes Hosea 6:6, "For I desire faithful love and not sacrifice, the knowledge of God rather than burnt offerings."

It is important to note that Mark and Luke do not record Jesus telling them to go and learn Hosea 6:6, but this fits in with Matthew's method of writing his Gospel as he often quotes the Old Testament. The last part of the verse reads, "And the knowledge of God more than burnt offerings."

Remember the book of Hosea is about mercy and kindness that is given to one who did not deserve it. God told Hosea to go and marry a prostitute as a sign to Israel of God's faithful keeping of the covenant and love for her even though she had forsaken the Lord. Hosea went to his wife who had rejected him, and he bought her from the slave block, redeeming her to himself.

It is a beautiful and apt description of God's love for a rebellious people. The LORD called Israel back to Himself even though Israel had played the harlot by worshipping other gods.

The Pharisees in Jesus' day had missed the whole point of the story of Hosea. They were so concerned with the scruples of the law that they missed the mandate from God to go after and help those who had broken the law, not condemn them. That is why Jesus told them to go and read it.

They missed the primary teaching in the Old Testament passage from Hosea: **God loves people more than anything**. He would rather us extend mercy, undeserved love and favor toward others than perform some religious duty to fulfill a law. Jesus emphasized service over sacrifice and relationship over ritual.

Here you have a vivid contrast between One who knows the heart of God and is living in that love and others who have forgotten the primary theological fact that God is love.

In many of our churches the same thing has happened. We have forgotten our purpose, which is to introduce lost, hurting people to Jesus Christ, and to extend mercy to them. We have become Pharisees, more concerned with keeping our brand of religion over ministering to hurting people on their way to hell. When we become legalists and turn inward, we lose our outward focus toward the unbeliever.

In the last part of Matthew 9:13, Jesus says, "For I didn't come to call the righteous, but sinners." He is not calling the Pharisees righteous. In fact, in Matthew 5:20, Jesus says, "For I tell you, unless your righteousness surpasses that of the scribes and Pharisees, you will never get into the kingdom of heaven."

Rather, Jesus is simply making his point of defining His Messianic mission, to seek and to save the lost. Jesus knew all were sinners and that "There is none righteous, no, not one" (Romans 3:10).

Carson makes an excellent point of interpretation when he writes, "By implication those who do not see themselves in the light of Jesus' mission not only fail to grasp the purpose of His coming but exclude themselves from the kingdom's blessings."[100]

LESSONS TO BE LEARNED FROM THIS EVANGELISTIC ENCOUNTER THAT JESUS HAD WITH MATTHEW.

MAJOR ON THE MISSION.

We are to go after the sinners and love them and share the Gospel with them, just as Jesus did. We are to seek the lost, not exclude them as the Pharisees did. We must always resist the spiritual gravitational pull to hang around those like us and shun unbelievers. I was so proud of our church at an event recently. Instead of getting in holy huddles, most spent time with guests and new people. This is so important, especially on Sundays!

FLEE PHARISAISM.

Stay humble and hungry for God. The best deterrent to avoid being like the very people that criticized Jesus is to love and help people. Tell people about Jesus. This will make you humble and very dependent upon God and leave no room for you to complain and be upset with what you do not have.

FOCUS ON THE ONE.

Call on people to give their lives to Christ. The Gospel message demands that we give people the opportunity to respond. Some will say no, but others like Matthew are ready and they will say yes. Thom Rainer has shown in his research that there are about 160 million lost people in the USA. He says 43 million would be open to attending a Bible study or going to church if you invited them and get this, 17 million would accept Jesus as their Savior if you only shared with them and gave them the opportunity! [101]

CHAPTER 11

THE CENTURION

"Lord," the centurion replied,
"I am not worthy to have you come under my roof.
But just say the word, and my servant will be healed.
For I too am a man under authority,
having soldiers under my command.
I say to this one, 'Go,' and he goes;
and to another, 'Come,' and he comes;
and to my servant, 'Do this!' and he does it."
Hearing this, Jesus was amazed and said to those following him,
"Truly I tell you , I have not found anyone in Israel
with so great a faith."

—MATTHEW 8:8-10

There are two accounts of the centurion and his interaction with our Lord. They are found in Matthew 8:5-13 and Luke 7:1-10. We will look closely at Matthew's account.

There is a difference in the two accounts. They are clearly referring to the same event, but a noticeable difference is easily recognizable. In Matthew's account, the centurion himself comes to Jesus and pleads with Him, but in Luke's account he sent servants who speak to Jesus.

Your approach to Scripture is critical at this point. If you approach the Bible, as many do today, contending that it is a flawed, human book, then you will find errors. But if you approach Scripture with humility and trust God that His Word is truth without any mixture of error, then you will find an answer to the alleged errors, discrepancies, or problem areas.

My approach to Scripture is this: if there seems to be a problem, I need to study further instead of casting some premature judgment on the Word of God. I call this a humble approach to hermeneutics, which is simply the art of interpretation.

There are a couple of possible reasons for the differences. One is that both are correct; that Matthew records a later visit by the centurion after he had sent the elders to speak to Jesus on behalf of his sick servant. [102]

The second is an interpretation that I came across from D.A. Carson, G. Campbell Morgan, and James Haley. These commentators state that it is the same event recorded two different ways.

Luke's account is correct that the centurion sent the elders on his behalf. Matthew records it as the centurion himself because as Carson states, "Matthew, following his tendency to condense, makes no mention of the servants in order to lay the greater emphasis on faith according to the principle...('he who acts by another acts himself')—a principle the centurion's argument implies in Matthew 8:8-9." [103]

Haley states as examples the time Zebedee's wife, James and John's mother, asked Jesus if her sons could sit at His right hand in Matthew 20:20; but in Mark 10:35 it is James and John who make the request themselves. He also uses the example of where in 2 Samuel 12:9, David is said to have killed Uriah "with the sword of the people of Ammon." David ordered him to be killed, but it was the Ammonites who physically killed Uriah.

Haley concludes, "Nothing is more common than that figure of speech by which we attribute to the man himself any act which he has either directly or indirectly procured to be done."[104]

Matthew 8:5 and Luke 7:2 both mention the centurion, who was a Roman soldier, a Gentile, with one hundred soldiers under his authority. The centurions were "the military backbone throughout the empire, maintaining discipline and executing orders."[105]

This particular centurion, who most likely served under Herod Antipas, the tetrarch or ruler of Galilee and Perea, came to Jesus or sent the elders of the Jewish community to Jesus to beg for his servant's healing.

This centurion had some good qualities. The Jews regarded him highly because he loved the Jewish people and had built a synagogue for them (Luke 7:5). They deemed him worthy of Jesus' time and attention, but he did not deem himself worthy (Matthew 8:8). He was a humble man even though he was in a prominent position as a centurion.

Also, Jesus gave him an incredibly high compliment by saying the man had great faith (Matthew 8:10). Another interesting thing about this soldier was the compassion he had for one of his own sick servants. *Doulos* is the word Luke uses for the servant, a household slave. [106]

We see in Matthew 8:8-9 that the man was genuinely humble. He actually personifies many of the Beatitudes found in Matthew 5:3-10. He says he is a man under authority. He is submissive to the authorities over him and ultimately the emperor himself.

Morgan points out that as a Roman soldier he was completely under the state's authority. "His time was not his own. His dress was chosen for him. His food was chosen for him. By the law of

Rome, no Roman soldier could hold any possessions."[107]

He also tells Jesus that he is a man in authority, as seen in verse 9. "He was under authority, and was therefore in authority. The authority he exercised over his soldiers was his submission to the authority over him."[108]

The centurion demonstrated an understanding of who Jesus was by using the analogy of the Roman system of authority. He spoke and his orders were obeyed because of who he represented, the Roman Emperor himself. He merely needed to say the word and it would happen. Carson states, "A foot soldier who disobeyed would not be defying a mere centurion but the emperor, Rome itself, with all its imperial majesty and might."[109]

The centurion applied this to Jesus. He merely needed to say the word and his servant would be healed because Jesus was under God's authority and vested with God's authority. Carson says, "So that when Jesus spoke, God spoke. To defy Jesus was to defy God;...This analogy, though not perfect, reveals an astonishing faith that recognizes that Jesus needed neither ritual, magic, or any other help; His authority was God's authority, and His word effective because it was God's word."[110]

In Matthew 8:10, Jesus marveled or wondered. This is the same word used in Mark 6:6, "And he was amazed at their unbelief." It is the Greek word *thaumazo*, which means to admire.

JESUS IS GREATLY IMPRESSED OR DISPLEASED BY THE FAITH WE EXHIBIT.

This is a constant lesson that I am trying to learn. Notice the word of approval and commendation Jesus gives to this Roman, a Gentile, a soldier of the state. Jesus says not only that he had faith, but that he had great faith.

The centurion had a clear understanding of who Jesus was, but he went further and acted on that understanding, without proof, and that is faith! The Gentile Roman centurion lacked the Jewish background and heritage that would equip him to understand the Messiah. Yet he demonstrated great faith and insight into the person and authority of Jesus, and this is impressive. [111]

Jesus says in Matthew 8:11-12 that many will come from various places and join the patriarchs in the kingdom of heaven. The "many" are the Gentiles. And "the sons of the kingdom" are the Jews who see themselves as going to heaven by right or heritage, because of who they are. [112]

However, they will not be in heaven but in the opposite of heaven. That is the destiny of eternal hell, which Jesus describes as a place of darkness and weeping and gnashing of teeth. The definite article "the" precedes the words weeping and gnashing in the Greek New Testament. This adds significance and solemnity to what He is saying. The words were graphic and shocking to Jesus' hearers, just as they are shocking to many today.

Jesus tells them, as He does us, through the written Word of God that there is a hell and that some Jews, not all Jews, will go there. **If this is true of Jews, then undoubtedly it is true of those of other religions. Admittance to heaven is not granted based on race, religion, or any other factor. It is solely based on simple faith and belief.**

After this, Jesus answered this man's request for the healing of the servant: "Then Jesus told the centurion, 'Go. As you have believed, let it be done for you.' And his servant was healed that very moment'" (Matthew 8:13).

How deeply do you care for others?

Notice Jesus' love for the centurion and then the centurion's love for his servant. In Matthew 8:7, Jesus says, "I will come and heal him."

Think about that. No one who ever lived was as busy or as fatigued as much as Jesus Christ, yet He cared for and loved others.

Kent Hughes in his book, *Disciplines of a Godly Man*, writes, "A glance at the Gospels reveals that He barely had any time for Himself unless He stole away...It has been said that the world is run by tired men, and it is true. Likewise, the Christian world is ministered to by tired people...Show me a great church and I will show you some tired people, both up front and behind the scenes, because greatness depends on a core of people who are willing to put out as the situation demands...We will never do great things for God without the willingness to extend ourselves for the sake of the gospel even when bone-tired." [113]

In Matthew 8:5, the centurion pled with Jesus on behalf of his servant. Luke 7:2 reveals this centurion's love and concern for his servant, saying that he was "dear to him."

May we be like Jesus Christ, and also follow the example of this centurion, genuinely loving and caring for people, being an advocate for them, and going out of our way for those who need us.

Does Jesus marvel at your faith?

In Matthew 8:10 we read that Jesus marveled at this man's faith and called it great. "Hearing this, Jesus was amazed and said to those following him, 'Truly I tell you, I have not found anyone in Israel with so great a faith.'"

Does Jesus marvel at the way we trust and obey Him? Does He call our faith great?

There are two key words I want you to associate with this encounter of Jesus Christ and the Roman centurion—humility and faith. He humbled himself before Christ and understood who he was. Moreover, he understood who Jesus was. He believed that Jesus was sent by God and empowered by God and that all He had to do was say the word and his servant would be healed. There is no hesitancy in his request. He asked totally believing it would come to pass because of the authority and power vested in the One to whom the request was made.

Effectiveness in living the Christian life is also tied up in these same two words—**humility and faith**. We have to continue to humble ourselves before God and place our total trust in Him. He will bless, as He is attracted to weakness and faith.

Jesus tells him in verse 13, "Go. As you have believed, let it be done for you."

Those words spoke to my heart. We know the man's faith was large, because Jesus granted his request according to his faith. The servant was healed. How many tremendous things could God do through us if we truly believed Him and did not doubt?

JESUS BELIEVED IN HELL. DO YOU?

Jesus gives a descriptive statement about hell in Matthew 8:12: "But the sons of the kingdom will be thrown into the outer darkness where there will be weeping and gnashing of teeth."

Many do not believe in hell today, and many Christians live their lives like they do not believe the lost are going to hell, but Jesus did believe in hell.

Part of the motivation for Christ to love and share and go was based upon His knowledge of the reality and harshness of the place He created called hell. According to Matthew 25:41, He created it for the devil and his angels. Many will go there based on their rejection of Jesus Christ.

We have completed a textual analysis of Matthew 8:5-13 and also looked at the parallel reading in Luke 7:1-10. How has God spoken to you through His Word?

For some, your spiritual decision or next step in your walk with God is to humble yourself before God and simply believe in Him. You know the Lord, now you have to begin really walking with the Lord. One of the ways you can do this is be sensitive to the ones God will bring in your path today, or this week. Be like Jesus and this Roman centurion in our text and slow down and speak, help, serve, simply care.

FOR
THE
ONE

CHAPTER 12

THE SYRO-PHOENICIAN WOMAN

"Then Jesus replied to her,
"Woman, your faith is great.
Let it be done for you as you want."
And from that moment
her daughter was healed.

—MATTHEW 15:28

The story of the Syro-Phoenician woman is recorded in Matthew 15:21-28 and Mark 7:24-30. We will study Matthew's account. This text has some difficult passages to understand which we will explore. It is good to grapple with the tough texts, studying them and interpreting them to the best of our ability. One of the reasons I enjoy preaching the Bible is that it forces all of us to deal with tough passages. As a result, we learn more and are in a better position to answer those who have questions.

Jesus retreats to the region of Tyre and Sidon, two cities located on the Mediterranean Sea about fifty miles northwest of Galilee. Morgan writes, "The journey which Jesus took to reach the region was one of at least fifty miles over mountainous country, and almost impassable roads." [114]

Morris tells us that "Sidon was about twenty-five miles north of Tyre, and that city was much the same distance from Jesus' Galilean haunts, so this represents a considerable journey on foot. The round trip could have taken months." [115]

Having been to Israel, I can appreciate even more this statement. Why did Jesus go to this Gentile region? We are not told specifically, but ultimately it was to engage in a ministry assignment given to Him by the Father. Dr. Wessell, in his commentary on Mark 7:24 says, "This suggests that He went there to get out of the public eye, perhaps to rest and prepare Himself spiritually for what He knew lay ahead of Him." [116]

Mark 7:24 says that, "He too could not be hidden, He could not escape notice. A Canaanite woman approached Him (Matthew 15:22)." Mark 7:26 describes her as a "Gentile, a Syrophoenician by birth." It is interesting to note that Matthew points out that she is a Canaanite.

Canaanites were some of the archenemies of the Jews in the past. This woman's religious background was steeped in the worship of the god of the Syrophoenicians, which was the goddess Astarte or Asheroth, the goddess of beauty. But the Greeks influenced this region, which led to the people and their worship degenerating into the worship of anything beautiful with no inhibition. "The worship of beauty had become the worship of everything thought desirable, within human personality, of which life was capable. All that is undoubtedly suggested by the declaration of the evangelist that this woman was a Syrophoenician." [117]

You can feel the pathos in her cry of desperation for Jesus to help her. One way to translate the verb "cried out" (Greek *kraugazo*) in Matthew 15:22 is scream. Her gods of beauty and pleasure could not help her at her hour of greatest need. She demonstrates some knowledge of the concept of the Hebrew Messiah by calling Jesus "the Son of David". His fame no doubt had spread to this region and the woman made her way to Jesus when she heard that He was in the vicinity. Her reason for coming to Jesus was because her daughter was demon-possessed. I believe this woman had heard of Jesus and she believed on Him. We also read in Matthew 15:22 that she calls Him Lord.

Jesus did not answer her initially. I think He did so for two reasons. **He would test the woman's faith and He would test the disciples to see their reaction to the woman.**

It is very important to understand these two things. With Christ, school was always in session for the disciples. He wasted not a minute on them, even while on a brief vacation. In Matthew 15:23, we see that the disciples wanted Jesus to send her away. Why? Did she bother them? Perhaps they were concerned that she would bother Jesus while He was trying to rest. Some believe that the disciples are asking Jesus to send her away healed.

Jesus tells her that He was sent to the lost sheep of the house of Israel. Carson quotes R.V.G. Tasker, pointing out that Jesus was limited by His physical humanity, and thus He was to focus on the primary target, the Jewish people. Carson states, "The kingdom must first be offered to them [the Jewish people]. The thought is like John 4:22: 'Salvation is from the Jews.' The Samaritan woman, like this Canaanite woman, had to recognize this—even if a time was coming when true worship would transcend such categories (John 4:23-26)." [118]

We see in Matthew 15:25 that this lady demonstrates faith and a clear belief in Jesus Christ. She calls Him Lord for the second time and now worships Him. The imperfect tense is used to describe her kneeling in worship. She *continued* to worship Him.

Jesus responded to her with an analogy in Matthew 15:26. The word for dogs here is the word not for the wild despised dog, but the word for household pets. Still, Jesus is making a distinction between Jew and Gentile. Salvation is of the Jews. The Messiah will come from the Hebrews, from the loins of Abraham, and in his loins all the nations of the earth will be blessed (Genesis 12:3). He will be from the tribe of Judah and the root or offspring of David.

In Romans 1:16, Paul says the Gospel is for all, for the Jew first and also for the Greek:

"For I am not ashamed of the gospel, because it is the power of God for salvation to everyone who believes, first to the Jew, and also to the Greek."

I like William Barclay's interpretation of verse 26, "We can be quite sure that the smile on Jesus' face and the compassion in his eyes robbed the words of all insult and bitterness." [119]

Former FBI hostage negotiator, Chris Voss, points out, "UCLA psychology professor Albert Mehrabian created the 7-38-55 rule. That is, only seven percent of a message is based on the words while thirty-eight percent comes from the tone of voice and fifty-five percent from the speaker's body language and face." [120]

The woman responds with a word of wit and faith in verse 27:

"'Yes, Lord,' she said, 'yet even the dogs eat the crumbs that fall from their masters' table.'"

Morgan points out that Jesus is dealing with her like this because He knows deep down she has this kind of faith. His method of dealing with her is indeed different than any other encounter. In fact, all of His encounters are different, because the people with whom He dealt were all different. However, He knew and loved each one. Morgan says of her response in verse 27, "that was the point when her faith reached its ultimate, and gained its victory...Thus all His method was vindicated as her faltering faith had persevered, until it had become victorious faith."[121]

In verse 28, Jesus says "O, woman." "O" is used only two times in Matthew and "woman" is not a harsh word but "Jesus is here using it in granting her request (he uses it also in his words to his mother from the cross, John 19:26)."[122] He points out her great faith. Not her rationale, her wit, or her ability to state her case. He acknowledged her faith.

Her faith enabled her to make the statements she made and present the case she did for her daughter. She admitted that Jesus came to the Jew first and that she was not a Jew. But she cast herself on the mercy of God and believed. Because of this she was blessed and her petition granted. D. A. Carson gives this lady a great compliment when he writes, "As does Paul in Romans 9-11, the woman preserves Israel's historical privilege over against all radical idealization or spiritualization of Christ's work, yet perceives that grace is freely given to the Gentiles."[123]

Note these four lessons or points of application from this story of Jesus' encounter with the Gentile woman, the Syrophoenician:

1. DIVINE SILENCES AND DELAYS DO NOT MEAN DIVINE INDIFFERENCE.

Look at verse 23. "But He answered her not a word." That grabs your attention. The reason He did not answer was, as we noticed earlier, two-fold.

He would test her faith and He would also test the faith of the disciples. It was not because Jesus was tired or showing prejudice against her. As we stated before with Christ, class was always in session for His disciples.

I thought about a statement my pastor in seminary made. For four years I sat under one of the best Bible expositors in the country. During the week, I went to school full-time and worked at night as a janitor. On Sundays I listened and learned.

My pastor said it well, "Divine delays do not mean divine indifference." **In other words, if you ask God for something and He does not respond immediately, that does not mean He has not heard you or that He does not care.** He hears our cries for help and mercy and in His time, not ours, He will answer.

This story reminds me of John 11:3, 6, 14-15. By the time Jesus arrived, it was four days after the initial request for Him to come and heal Lazarus. We must remember God is always perfect in everything He does. You may not be able to see it at the moment, but He will answer and it will be for your best according to Romans 8:28:

"We know that all things work together for the good of those who love God, who are called according to his purpose."

The Bible says *all things!* I heard Pastor Caleb Turner make a statement that really spoke to me. I sent it to my family, shared it with my church family, and I want to share it with you. With reference to King David hiding out in a cave from Saul, Pastor Turner said, "Because God loves us, He has us where He wants us."

One of the godliest men in church history was Pastor George Mueller. He is known for being a man of prayer, as well as for his work among the children in his orphanages in Bristol, England.

Mueller prayed specifically for two men for fifty years. Someone asked him if he really thought the two men he had prayed for would be converted.

Mueller said, "Do you think God would have kept me praying

all these years if He did not intend to save them?"

Both of these men were eventually saved. One was converted just prior to Mueller's death and the other man just after his death. [124]

2. DEAL WITH EACH PERSON DIFFERENTLY.

One of the things that stands out as we study the way Jesus dealt with people in the New Testament is that He treated all people with respect and love, but never in the same manner. The reason is because people are not the same.

We need to be sensitive to the Holy Spirit and follow His guidance while we are ministering to them, especially as we witness.

With some we need to be a little more creative, as Jesus was here with this woman. With others, we need to be more conversational. If we will pray for opportunities to share Christ, and depend on the Holy Spirit's power and help, He will indeed grant us opportunities to witness. He will also give us the words to say and the way we need to say it.

3. DETERMINATION AND PERSEVERANCE ARE ALWAYS REWARDED.

At first Jesus was silent and the disciples were urging her to leave. When Jesus did speak to her, He tested her, so what would this woman do? She could have given up and left, as so many people do today. But she drew near.

She was shouting, perhaps because she was at a distance. Notice what Matthew 15:25 says, "Then she came."

She was no longer at a distance; she was near. She did not

turn away and give up, but she walked toward her Answer with determination. When school gets hard, some quit; when churches raise the bar of expectations, some find another one; when the spouse turns out to be human and not perfect after all, some look for another one. This is the way of most of humanity—when the going gets tough, they quit.

But not this woman! She believed and persisted in her request. Moreover, she recognized Jesus for who He was and she worshiped Him. She had grit and wit!

She reminds me of the lady in Luke 18:1-8 who kept on asking the judge to give her justice and he finally did, not because he feared God or cared for man, but because he did not want to be bothered by her anymore.

The lady in Matthew 15 was a determined lady; she would persevere out of love for her daughter. If there is one message I could ingrain in my family, friends, and church it is this: Do not quit; God rewards and blesses those who keep on going.

There was a great race on August 7, 1954, in Vancouver, Canada, between the two fastest men in the world. Roger Banister and John Landy were the only sub-four milers in the world. John Landy had a large lead going into the third lap, so Bannister poured it on and caught him. Their pace was even at the final lap. But Landy made a tragic error. He could not see Bannister and so he decided to look back to find out how close he was. When he did Bannister sped past and beat him by only a few yards. [125]

Child of God, don't look back, retreat, give up; rather, keep your focus on Christ and do what you know is the right thing to do. Best-selling author Andy Andrews signed one of his books for me, and inside the cover I noticed he had one word written. He simply wrote the word "Persevere!" I encourage you to do the same—keep pressing forward and trusting God. He sees.

He will come through for you, just do not give up!

4. JESUS RESPONDS TO OUR FAITH.

In Matthew 15:28, our Lord commends her for trusting in Him. He grants her request as a result of her faith. This woman persisted in the face of difficult odds. She would not back down because the need was so great. She wanted Jesus to heal her daughter of the tormenting demon. He did just that, but only after she asked, persisted, and believed. I wonder how close we come to seeing our prayers answered, but we give up and miss out.

I encourage you to look straight ahead and do not hesitate in your walk with God. Believe as this woman believed. God may be silent right now but that does not mean He does not know or He does not care. He knows. He cares. Trust Him.

FOR THE ONE

CHAPTER 13

THE WOMAN IN JOHN 8

When Jesus stood up, he said to her,
"Woman, where are they?
Has no one condemned you?"
"No one, Lord," she answered.
"Neither do I condemn you," said Jesus.
"Go, and from now on do not sin anymore."

—JOHN 8:10-11

I have always been intrigued and blessed by John 8:1-11.
I understand that the older Greek manuscripts do not have this
passage of Scripture, but it is in many manuscripts. It is also in
the writings of great church fathers like Augustine and Jerome.
In *The Believer's Study Bible*, it says, "There is every probability
that the story represents an actual event in the life of Jesus." [126]
I believe the story is true and valid. It seems that every time
I read this amazing story, I learn something new.

When studying the life of Jesus, keep in mind these
thoughts—**He loved the Father and all He did was in response
to the Father's will for His life**. John 5:19 says, "Jesus replied,
'Truly I tell you, the Son is not able to do anything on his own,

but only what He sees the Father doing. For whatever the Father does, the Son likewise does these things.'"

Jesus was a disciple maker. You see Him throughout His life in the Gospels pouring into the twelve Apostles and teaching them how to live.

Jesus loved people, all people. Throughout the Gospels you see Him helping, healing, teaching, ministering, and serving.

Jesus was kind toward sinners but harsh toward religious, mean people. He comforted the afflicted and afflicted the comfortable. He was constantly loving the unlovable and the outcasts, and as He did, He came in the crosshairs of those who should have been loving and helping the people. The religious aristocrats, however, would rather kill Jesus and keep their brand of religion than submit to His Lordship and follow Him.

In John 8, you see all of these characteristics of the life and ministry of Jesus at work. And as you read it, be open to the Holy Spirit speaking to you and comforting you if you are afflicted and afflicting you if you are too comfortable.

Let's look at seven important questions:

1. WHO IS SHE?

We do not have a name, but she was someone's daughter, a Jewish lady most likely, and she made a mistake, a big mistake.

All sin is sin, no doubt, but the effects of some sins are far greater than others. Society and the law will forgive you easily for stealing a piece of candy from the store, but not so much if you steal a woman's husband. She was guilty but so was he! We don't see him being brought before the people, but he is just as guilty.

One of the Ten Commandments clearly says, "Do not commit adultery" (Exodus 20:14). The Law stipulated the punishments for such an egregious act of committing adultery.

Deuteronomy 22:23-24 states, "If there is a young woman who is a virgin engaged to a man, and another man encounters her in the city and sleeps with her, take the two of them out to the gate of that city, and stone them to death with stones, the young woman because she did not cry out in the city, and the man because he humbled his neighbor's wife; so you shall put away the evil from among you." [127]

Carson writes, "Although capital punishment by stoning is still meted out today in some Muslim countries for the offence of adultery, there is little evidence that it was carried out very often in first-century Palestine, especially in urban areas." [128]

But the authorities were not as interested in justice to the woman as much as they were inflamed with revenge on Jesus. They do not even bring the man to be judged. I think they may have even had this woman set up. She was but a pawn in their evil hands to use to try and trick Jesus, so they could remove Him.

There are many women today who are being grossly taken advantage of, and who are trapped in sexual slavery. Every one of them is someone's daughter, a precious daughter of the King of Heaven, and worthy not of abuse, but to be highly cherished and valued.

My wife Ashley and I watched the movie *Priceless* about this very topic of sex slavery, with Joel David Smallbone of the band *For King and Country* playing the lead role. It is very well done. On Thanksgiving Day our church, Great Hills Baptist Church in Austin, Texas, hosted a Turkey Trot/Walk, with all of the proceeds going to Refuge, a sex trafficking ministry in the Austin area.

The religious people cared nothing for this woman whose story is in John 8. They did not care about her hurt, embarrassment, the pain of what she was experiencing—they only wanted a stone for justice with no olive branch of mercy.

Primarily, however, they were out for blood—the death of Jesus. We see that Jesus treated her far differently than these religious men.

2. WHAT DID SHE DO?

She committed adultery, thereby breaking one of the Ten Commandments. It was wrong then and it is wrong today. It matters because God told us not to do it. It also matters because it destroys trust and it can absolutely destroy relationships.

Jesus raised the bar for His followers in the Sermon on the Mount when He said in Matthew 5:27-28, "You have heard that it was said to those of old, 'You shall not commit adultery.' But I say to you that whoever looks at a woman to lust for her has already committed adultery with her in his heart."

Jesus loved this lady but not her sin. He was going to die for her sins and all the sins of the world. We know He did not approve because He told her later in the story to go and sin no more. He called it what it was, *sin*, a violation of the command of God.

3. WHERE IS THE GUY?

We do not read about the other guilty party; by the way to do this sin of adultery you have to have another person! He is nowhere to be found, which I find appalling. Remember, however, that those who are devising this plan are not concerned with true justice but revenge. They wanted to catch and kill Jesus.

Revenge will make you do stupid things. You will not think clearly, and you will use others and act in ungodly ways, all in the pursuit of getting even.

4. WHY ARE RELIGIOUS PEOPLE SO MEAN?

We read often of this religious group called the scribes and Pharisees. Carson writes, "The scribes were the recognized students and expositors of the law of Moses, but so central was the law in the life and thought of first-century Palestinian Jews that the scribes came to assume something of the roles of lawyer, ethicist, theologian, catechist, and jurist. Most of them, but certainly not all, were Pharisees by conviction."[129]

They were the religious leaders and were tasked with shepherding the people of God, the pastors of the Jews, the ones who taught in the synagogues and led the people in ways that honored God and the law.

However, they became so engrossed in the letter of the law that they forgot about God and helping people. I know they were extremely threatened by Jesus because the people loved Him. They were jealous, and we all know the evil done under the influence of the green-eyed monster. Unchecked jealousy will eventually turn into unbridled revenge.

They truly thought they had a "gotcha" moment where they had Jesus trapped. If He does not consent and have her stoned, then He disobeys Moses; if He does have her killed, then Rome will come after Him because it was their sole right to execute.

Be careful of religious zeal that is more concerned with dos and don'ts and has little concern about people or what they are experiencing. You hurt far more than you know, and your reach is far greater than you could imagine.

Reading over the text again recently, I saw something I had never seen before in John 8:9. The religious leaders had more than a few people with them and included in this group were young, aspiring theologians and future rabbis. The older ones were indoctrinating the younger group and not in a good way.

Our influence as leaders always impacts either for good or evil.

I was listening to a podcast recently where Dr. William Havlicek was answering questions about his biography of the famous painter Vincent Van Gogh. I was so impressed with the interview that I bought the book.

Ashley and I went to the Museum of Modern Art in New York City and viewed paintings by Monet and Van Gogh, especially the *Starry Night*. This painting is worth over one hundred million dollars! Havlicek said that Van Gogh was definitely a Christian with a testimony of God's redeeming grace in his life. He even became a pastor in Belgium among coal miners and loved his people and dressed like the common laborer. However, his attire did not settle well with the religious elite and they rebuked him for what he wore, so he left the ministry.

No doubt God brought good out of this evil done to him, but what could have been the effect of his pastoral ministry if the modern day Pharisees had not criticized him? Like a pig to the mud, the religious zealot with little understanding of grace will criticize every single time.

5. WHAT DID JESUS WRITE?

In John 8:6, 8, Jesus wrote something on the ground. "Jesus stooped down and started writing on the ground with his finger...Then he stooped down again and continued writing on the ground."

Of course, while this interests me, there is really no way of knowing what He wrote, but we can speculate. I have read that He wrote the sins of the people who had stones in their hands, or He wrote a cross in the dirt, or that He wrote Jeremiah 17:13, "O LORD, the hope of Israel, all who forsake You shall be ashamed. Those who depart from Me shall be written in the earth, because they have forsaken the LORD, the fountain of living waters."

One of our church staff said that she believes that Jesus wrote John 12:47 in the sand, "If anyone hears my words and doesn't keep them, I do not judge him; for I did not come to judge the world but to save the world."

6. WHAT DID JESUS SAY?

While we do not know what He wrote, we surely know what He said, for John gives the response to us. Soak in these words of Jesus in John 8:7, 10-12:

"When they persisted in questioning him, he stood up and said to them, "The one without sin among you should be the first to throw a stone at her."

—JOHN 8:7

"When Jesus stood up, he said to her, 'Woman, where are they? Has no one condemned you?'

'No one, Lord,' she answered.

'Neither do I condemn you,' said Jesus. 'Go, and from now on do not sin anymore.'

Jesus spoke to them again: 'I am the light of the world. Anyone who follows me will never walk in the darkness but will have the light of life.'"

—JOHN 8:10-12

Jesus disarmed the religious Pharisees with one simple question. In verse 10, the religious accusers had all left, but Jesus was still there, and I believe the crowds were still there. They probably were so impressed and pleased with how Jesus put the scribes and Pharisees in their place.

Jesus responds with two questions. The answers to both are obvious, but He wants her and all of us to contemplate and to think deeply.

Where are the accusers? Well, they had left. "Has no one condemned you?" There was no more condemnation from them.

Jesus' words in verse 11 are classic, brilliant, and full of grace and truth. In Matthew 5:17, Jesus said, "Do not think that I came to destroy the Law or the Prophets. I did not come to destroy but to fulfill."

John 1:14 says Jesus was full of grace and truth and we see this clearly here. Paul said in Ephesians 4:15 that we are to be "speaking the truth in love."

Look at verse 12. Jesus addresses the people mentioned in verse 2 who had come to hear Him teach until he was so rudely interrupted. Jesus is the light of the world. Light dispels darkness and brightens the path so all can see and travel safely.

I believe Jesus equates walking in darkness with what they had just witnessed by the actions of the religious leaders. It is so ironic that those who were supposed to be bearers of light to illuminate the path for people to travel spiritually were full of darkness, or as Jesus referred to them, blind guides. Matthew 23:24 states, "Blind guides, who strain out a gnat and swallow a camel!"

7. WILL JESUS FORGIVE ME?

The answer is a resounding yes! Jesus Christ came to forgive sinners, said the Apostle Paul In I Timothy 1:15. He states, "This is a faithful saying and worthy of all acceptance, that Christ Jesus came into the world to save sinners, of whom I am chief."

This woman in our story did not need a stone but she desperately needed grace. We are so often consumed with being right that we forget to be kind. We err either on the side of grace and say, "Oh, it (the sin) does not matter!" or we err on the side of law and we say, "Everything matters!" But Jesus was and is full of grace and truth.

What do you need today? Would you not agree that your greatest need is peace with God and with others? Jesus can grant this to you in full measure. Believe.

The only person Jesus cannot help is the person who thinks he needs no help. The religious Pharisees rejected Jesus because they thought they were fine and right with God. But they were far from God. They would not admit, repent, and believe in Jesus.

God will give bread and not a stone. He will in no way cast you out when you come to him.

CHAPTER 14

THE MAN WITH THE
WITHERED HAND

Then Jesus said to them,
"I ask you: Is it lawful to do good on the Sabbath or to do evil,
to save life or to destroy it?"
After looking around at them all,
he told him, "Stretch out your hand."
He did, and his hand was restored.

—LUKE 6:9-10

Whenever we study the life of Christ we will be challenged to be more caring, compassionate and giving. It is much easier and takes so much less effort to pass by those that hurt, or just say a prayer for them and move on. But the life of Jesus Christ demands much more from the people of God.

Some of you are like me in that you are very task-oriented

and you have your to-do list and you get much accomplished by staying focused on the task at hand. You relate to the old adage, "If you want to get something done, ask someone who is busy." You are busy, and you get much accomplished.

But what do you do when God tells you—depart from what you have in mind, and do what I have for you to do—What do you do then? Unfortunately, I have been known to delay or be disobedient when God changes my plans. But I want to do better. I never want to miss an opportunity when God leads me to encourage another person or share the Gospel with him or her.

Luke 6:6-11 reveals again the compassion of Jesus, the plight of those who are hurting, and also exposes the caustic, bitter antagonism of the religious leaders. We frequently see these three people or dynamics collide in the New Testament. And they will collide intensely again in our text in Luke 6. Jesus does not shy away from the hurting nor does He back away from a confrontation with the religious leaders of His day.

Let's analyze the **Setting**, the **Savior**, and finally some lessons from the **Story**:

1. THE SETTING — A MAN IN NEED (LUKE 6:6-8)

The story of the healing of the man with the withered hand is recorded in all three of the Synoptic Gospels—Matthew, Mark, and Luke.

In our text Jesus goes to a synagogue in Galilee to teach. A man was there and we are not given his name. But he is in church on the Sabbath to worship God. He did not come to church necessarily to be healed, but while at church that day something grand happened to him.

This man had a right hand that was withered. The Greek word

for withered is *xeros* and it means scorching, arid, and dry. [130] The word can also mean shriveled, atrophied, and useless. [131] The same word is used in John 5:3 with the man at the pool of Bethesda who was paralyzed.

We observe the religious aristocracy watching Jesus closely to see if He would heal on the Sabbath. The word translated *watched* is in the imperfect tense—continually they were watching Jesus. The word can also mean spy. [132]

They wanted to find an accusation against Him. The word translated *accusation* is the Greek word, *kategoria*, where we get the English word category. The word means complaint or a criminal charge. **They wanted to catch Jesus breaking one of their many codes, variations or categories of sins.**

What a sad existence; they were constantly absorbed with catching Jesus in some wrongdoing. Of course, that was a futile endeavor because He never sinned. What if they had used their energies on doing good rather than trying to harm or catch someone else doing something wrong?

Here we have a clash again between Jesus and the scribes and Pharisees. This is a study in contrasts. Jesus is loving and compassionate, but the others are not interested in helping hurting people in their pain.

Morgan writes, "The rulers did not know God, and when men do not know God they are always interested in trivialities,… When men know God, they know that the passion of His heart is ever full of understanding and mercy." [133]

Jesus read their minds. "But he knew their thoughts and told the man with the shriveled hand, 'Get up and stand here.' So he got up and stood there" (Luke 6:8).

The word translated "thoughts" is the Greek word *dialogismos*, from which we get dialogue and it means "internal discussion." [134] It's interesting that this is what Simeon said would happen in his prophecy regarding Jesus in Luke 2:35, "...that the thoughts of many hearts may be revealed."[135]

They were at church for all the wrong reasons, not to worship God or learn from Jesus' teaching; rather, they were there with vindictive motives. Jesus told the man to arise and stand and he did just that—he arose and stood as Jesus instructed him.

Why do you go to church? Is it to worship God, meet Jesus, and see Him transform lives? Or do you attend because it is your habit and you are not really expecting anything to happen? Or worse, do you go to church only to judge and criticize and catch the pastor or some other leader in a mistake?

To be in a church where God's Word is taught, where songs of praise are sung, and where people are saved, baptized, and discipled should be enough for you. This should render any urge you have to complain absolutely powerless.

2. THE SAVIOR—HELPING THE NEEDY (LUKE 6:9-11)

Jesus used the occasion as an object lesson for all in attendance that day, especially for the religious crowd. Look at Jesus' question, recorded in verse 9, "I ask you, is it lawful to do good on the Sabbath or to do evil, to save life or to destroy it?"

Notice that Jesus equates doing good with saving life and doing evil with destroying life. To have the power to do good and yet not do it is sin, as James 4:17 teaches, "So it is sin to know the good and yet not do it."

Mark 3:3 says that after Jesus asked the question, "they kept silent." For the religious Jews the observance of the Sabbath was paramount and a determining factor in one's righteousness. They had concluded that a non life-threatening case could wait until after the Sabbath. Jesus challenged that notion.

"Against these Pharisees and scribes, Jesus refuses to represent Sabbath observance as a litmus test for faithfulness to God. More fundamental for Him is God's design to save—a purpose that is...embodied in God's purpose for the Sabbath."[136]

Matthew 12:11-14 also gives an account of this story. Jesus gave them an analogy or comparison and made a powerful point:

"He replied to them, 'Who among you, if he had a sheep that fell into a pit on the Sabbath, wouldn't take hold of it and lift it out? A person is worth far more than a sheep; so it is lawful to do what is good on the Sabbath.'"

In Luke 6:10, Jesus looked around at the people. Then Jesus told the man to stretch out his hand. **He commanded him to do what was impossible**. This hand was withered, very possibly paralyzed, and he was unable to stretch it out, but Jesus commanded him to do so in faith.

Morgan writes, "As long as I am looking at myself, His commands are impossible, and unreasonable. But the moment I look at Him, I find they are both possible and reasonable. . . . As he in obedience made contact with the power of Christ, that power became his enablement. It was not a case of waiting to obey until there was a consciousness of healing. It was obedience to a word of command, and it was in that action of the will that contact was made with power."[137]

Notice the little statement "he did" in Luke 6:10. That is obedience, and God blessed him as God always honors obedience.

You would think the religious leaders would rejoice and give God praise for the healing, for the clear intervention of God in their midst. Instead, they reacted just the opposite—they were filled with rage (*anoia*)—madness, fury. They cannot believe their eyes that Jesus would dare do such a thing as heal on the Sabbath. They were furious; they were at their wits' end. [138]

3. THE STORY—SOME LESSONS LEARNED

These are important truths to glean from this encounter of Jesus Christ and the man with the withered hand:

1. WORSHIP WHILE YOU WAIT.

Be faithful and worship God, even in the midst of pain and difficulty. The man with the withered hand went to church to worship. If we wait until all is well before we serve God, worship, or witness, then we will never serve God, worship, or witness. We will always have some measure of difficulty in this life. Remember Matthew 6:33—seek first God's kingdom and righteousness and He will add all things to us.

2. IMPOSSIBILITIES BECOME POSSIBILITIES THROUGH CHRIST.

Obey God even though the command seems impossible to you. The man with the withered hand in the synagogue that day must have thought it a strange command, but he obeyed anyhow. He tried to do the impossible at Jesus' command.

Remember Luke 18:27 when Jesus said, "What is impossible with man is possible with God." When God commands you to do something, He always provides the ability to do it, but we have to trust in Him. Without Jesus we can do nothing, but with Him we can do all things! (Philippians 4:13).

"I am the vine, you are the branches. The one who remains in Me and I in him produces much fruit; because you can do nothing without Me."

—JOHN 5:15

3. BE A PART OF THE SOLUTION, NOT THE PROBLEM.

Had Jesus not healed the man with the withered hand, the religious leaders would have been fine with that.

How in the world could they reason that way in their minds, that it would be better to keep a religious law than to help someone in obvious need? Beware of those who do not rejoice when God does a mighty work. Associate with problem-solvers, not problem-makers.

4. CONFRONT MAN-MADE TRADITIONS THAT ARE UNBIBLICAL.

If God's Word comes into conflict with a tradition of man, then always choose the Word of God.

The Pharisees were so engrossed in their works religion that they could not see that God's Grace had personally stepped into their midst. Confrontation is never easy. God has given me quite a bit of it in my life because it stretches me completely and makes me even more dependent on Him.

5. REMEMBER YOUR MISSION—FOR THE ONE!

Over and over in the New Testament Jesus reminds us through precept and example that our purpose is to serve God by helping others. The religious people, of all people, the religious people, the leaders, the shepherds should have been the ones caring for and seeking ways to help this man, but they did not because they in their twisted theology concluded that it would be better for this man to suffer so they could keep a deeply-held tradition of man.

Jesus loves people. As His church, His followers today, we must also love people and do all in our power to love and minister to those in need.

I came across a story about a young boy who understands what it means to help those who hurt or are less fortunate. Casey Draper of Tuba City, New Mexico, and his mom were cleaning out his room and going through his toys. His mom suggested that he sell the toys and buy himself a really nice Christmas present. But Casey said he would rather use the money to buy presents for family members. On December 3, 2008, though, he changed his mind when he saw a Toys for Tots commercial. He decided he would sell his toys and buy new toys for those in need. Casey said, "Well, there's people out there that can't have Christmas or don't have Christmas." He sold his toys at a flea market and gave all the $179.50 to the Navajo Nation Toys for Tots. When Casey Draper did this, he was four years old! [139]

I encourage you to never let man's traditions or your personal preferences be confused with God's will. We are to concern ourselves more with substance than style. Our focus should not be that of the Pharisees who felt they had a monopoly on all the ways of God. Rather, we need to remember Christ and be passionate for loving and helping others, the ones He puts in our path.

FOR
THE
ONE

CHAPTER 15

MARY, THE MOTHER OF JESUS

When Jesus saw his mother and the disciple he loved
standing there, he said to his mother,
"Woman, here is your son."
Then he said to the disciple, "Here is your mother."
And from that hour the disciple took her into his home.

—JOHN 19:26-27

In John 19:26-27, we see that Jesus, as He was dying on the cross, takes care of His mother, Mary. She is the one before Him that He focuses on. It is an astounding demonstration of care and concern. The thing about this that staggers me is, even in the midst of horrible, excruciating pain, Jesus loves and provides for her.

It is one thing to be generous and help others or reach out to the one God places in front of us when things are rosy, life is good, and our health is excellent.. But it is such a different and far more stellar and wonderful thing when we can love and help others even in the very midst of our own suffering and agony.

Mary was a young lady when Gabriel appeared to her with the astonishing news in Luke 1:30-35:

Then the angel told her, "Do not be afraid, Mary, for you have found favor with God. Now listen, you will conceive and give birth to a Son, and you will name him Jesus. He will be great and will be called the Son of the Most High; and the Lord God will give Him the throne of His father David. He will reign over the house of Jacob forever, and His kingdom will have no end."

Mary asked the angel, "How can this be, since I have not had sexual relations with a man?"

The angel replied to her, "The Holy Spirit will come upon you, and the power of the Most High will overshadow you. Therefore, the Holy One to be born will be called the Son of God."

In a moment, Mary's life changed. She went from an engaged, or as they called it in the Bible, a betrothed young lady, probably a teenager, to being chosen by God and told, "You will bear a Son!" God chose her, and her life would never be the same. By all accounts we can deduce that she was a wonderful mother and loved her Son dearly. Jesus' brothers did not believe on Him until after the resurrection. But Mary knew who He was. You just don't have a child the way she did unless God intervenes!

There is much beauty in the midst of the ashes. There is a beautiful calm in the heart of extreme chaos. God can do some of His greatest work in us when we are at our lowest points. If we wait to serve God and give our best when all is well, then we will spend a good portion of our life ineffective and inactive for the things of God.

Why? It is a fact that a portion of our lives will be lived in mundane days and others in very dark and difficult days.

Herein lies one of the beauties of the Christian life and what is so attractive to those outside of Christ—the Holy Spirit within us empowers us to do what we could never do in our own strength!

We see that Jesus, John, and Mary moved forward with God the Father's redemptive plans during the crucible of pain.

D. A. Carson has some excellent insights into our text. He explains why Jesus' brothers did not take in their mom. He also expounds on how some have interpreted this text to mean that she had taken in John, thereby exalting her as the mother of the church:

"It is wonderful to remember that even as he hung dying on a Roman cross, suffering as the Lamb of God, Jesus took thought of and made provision for his mother. Some have found it surprising that Jesus' brothers did not take over this responsibility. But quite apart from the fact that they were at this point quite unsympathetic to their older brother (John 7:5), they may not even have been in Jerusalem: their home was in Capernaum (John 2:12)...

True enough, but this is not a legal scene. Jesus displays his care for his mother, as both she and the beloved disciple are passing through their darkest hour, on their way to full Christian faith. *From that time (høra, 'hour') on, from the 'hour' of Jesus' death/exaltation (John 2:4; 12:23; 17:1), this disciple took her into his home...*

Roman Catholic exegesis has tended not so much to see Mary coming under the care of the beloved disciple, as the reverse; and if the beloved disciple is also taken as an idealization of all true disciples, the way is cleared to think of Mary as the mother of the church." [140]

What does this passage say to you as you are reaching "the one"?

1. LOOK AT OTHERS AND UNDERSTAND THEIR DIFFICULTY IN THE MIDST OF YOUR OWN.

John 19:26 says, "When Jesus saw." Jesus saw Mary and John. He saw the looks in their eyes and the great grief and pain they were experiencing. We really cannot fathom the pain Jesus was experiencing in this moment, not only the physical pain of being nailed to a cross, but also the emotional pain of being ridiculed and rejected by the very people He created. But there was an even deeper pain, and that was the separation He had never experienced from God the Father, as He who knew no sin became sin for us so we could become the righteousness of God, as Paul states in 2 Corinthians 5:21.

Kristen, a woman in our church, was in a car accident and she asked the woman in the other car, who was in obvious distress, if she could pray for her. The lady asked Kristen, "Why would you want to pray for me after I hit you?" Kristen said, "Accidents happen, I am glad you were not hurt, and I believe the Lord is leading me to pray for you." She agreed and Kristen prayed for her and gave her one of our church cards with an invitation to come and visit on Sunday. Kristen wrote me in a text, "Yes my car is damaged, yes it's frustrating, but the potential eternal impact on her was well worth the minor inconvenience."

2. SPEAK TO THE PAINFUL SITUATION.

John 19:26 also says, "He said to His mother." I got a text from one of our church members telling me he had come through his surgery and he was in pain. Then he sent another text right after this one and he wrote, "Witnessed to everyone, even a Buddhist. Praise God!"

3. GO A STEP FURTHER AND HELP.

In John 19:27, when Jesus told John that Mary was now his mother, John knew what this meant. He was to care for and provide for her just like she was his own biological mother. It is really amazing to me that Jesus goes to these great lengths while dying on a cross after all He had gone through!

Think about the scene John records for us in this text. Jesus is dying on the cross. Why? He is dying for your sins and mine. That fact is very clear when you read the New Testament. Romans 5:8 speaks to this divine love directly. He invites us to receive Him and His forgiveness. The way this happens is by repentance and faith; turning from sin to Jesus. He invites us to follow Him. We are to do as He did. If we His people were more like Him, this world would easily be reached with the Gospel.

Allow me to remind you to allow Jesus' actions to motivate you to do the same. Even in the midst of your hurt and pain, look at others and understand their hurt and pain. Speak to the person in pain. By speaking you are now taking your mind off of *you* and addressing another person's plight. And finally, yes, even in the midst of your difficulty, improve the situation, make it better for the one who is before you, who needs a special touch of grace.

FOR THE ONE

FOR
THE
ONE

CHAPTER 16

RICH YOUNG RULER

Looking at him, Jesus loved him
and said to him, "You lack one thing:
Go, sell all you have and give to the poor,
and you will have treasure in heaven.
Then come, follow me."
But he was dismayed by this demand,
and he went away grieving,
because he had many possessions.

—MARK 10:17-22

Jesus looked upon others with compassion, loved them unconditionally, got involved in their lives, and gave His life away in service, eventually laying His life down on the cross for the sins of the world.

Jesus was humble and selfless. Philippians 2:5 tells us we should have the same mind as Jesus, "Let this mind be in you which was also in Christ Jesus."

We are never more like Christ than when we are investing in others and helping them on a physical, emotional, and especially spiritual level.

Let's look at how Jesus' interacts with the man described as rich, young, and a ruler. It is an intriguing story because the Lord gives this man something we would describe as tough love. He told the man what he needed to hear but certainly what he did not wish to hear.

It is good to keep in mind the setting of our text. Jesus has previously spent time with little children and blessed them in Mark 10:13-16. He told the crowd that whoever wants to go to heaven must be like a little child. A child, as we know, humbly trusts.

Next, we read of Jesus' encounter with the man known forever as the rich young ruler. All three Synoptic Gospels contain the story. It is in Matthew 19, Mark 10 and Luke 18. We will look at Mark's account.

In Mark 10:17, the rich young ruler who came to Jesus has been described by G. Campbell Morgan as:

1. DISCERNABLE—

He approached Jesus and recognized Him as a good teacher.

2. COURAGEOUS—

While other Jewish leaders avoided or rejected Jesus, he approached Him and spoke to Him. He may have been a ruler in the sense of a ruler or leader of a synagogue.

3. HUMBLE—

He knelt before Jesus.

4. HONEST OR RELIGIOUS—

He tried to keep the commandments.

5. UNFULFILLED—

The rich young ruler asked, "What shall I do to inherit eternal life?"[141]

Jesus engages the young man in Mark 10:18 by asking him a question:

"'Why do you call me good?' Jesus asked him. 'No one is good except God alone.'"

Jesus is not questioning His own deity, as some liberal scholars claim. In other places in Scripture, Jesus clearly identifies who He is. In John 8:58, He says, "Truly I tell you, before Abraham was, I am."

In John 3:16, Jesus says, "For God loved the world in this way: He gave his one and only Son, so that everyone who believes in him will not perish but have eternal life."

In John 14:6, He says, "I am the way, the truth, and the life. No one comes to the Father except through me."

This was in the third year of Jesus' ministry. Jesus' first year has been described as the year of obscurity; the second, the year of popularity; and the third, the year of hostility. Dr. Roy Fish states regarding Mark 10:18, "What was Jesus trying to do?... Jesus was trying to get the one who asked to recognize Him as God. Jesus said essentially, 'I am not good if I am not God. Don't compliment Me like this unless you admit that I am God.'"

John Calvin also interprets this verse in a similar way.[142] Perhaps Jesus is addressing the basic need of this man because this young man trusts in his own goodness. Jesus is showing him that only God is good, and he will never be good enough; he needs God's help.

William Lane states, "In calling into question the man's use of 'good,' Jesus' intention is not to pose the question of His own sinlessness or oneness with the Father, but to set in correct perspective the honor of God." [143]

In Mark 10:19-20, Jesus quotes the last six of the Ten Commandments, those dealing with mankind's relationship with his fellow man. The first four are about man's relationship to God. Jesus did not address the first four because this man was already violating the first commandment of the ten, "You shall have no other gods before Me" (Exodus 20:3).

The rich young ruler tells Jesus, "I have kept all these from my youth" (Mark 10:20). He may be around thirty years of age, and he says he has kept the Laws Jesus referenced. Youth here may refer to the age of twelve, the age when he was responsible for keeping the Law. [144]

Jesus looked at him and the Bible says, "Jesus loved him" (Mark 10:21). Then Jesus told him what he must do—replace his god of materialism with the One true God as the Lord of His life.

Jesus knew what the young man lacked and spoke the truth to him in love. He had to abandon all other gods and surrender his life to God in Christ. [145]

While studying this text, I wondered if perhaps Jesus is calling him out by questioning the man's usage of the word "good." He is God and He is good. The rich young ruler does not know God because he has another god in the One true God's rightful place. Perhaps Jesus wanted him to think about why he called Jesus good if he was not willing to follow Him and serve Him as God.

Jesus tells him to "go, sell...and give," and then to "come, follow me" (Mark 10:21). He was to repent and believe. He was to turn away from his god of money and by faith embrace Christ and follow Him.

Jesus does not call everyone to come after him in this command of selling all one has to follow Him. But whatever holds one back from following Christ, whether it is money, a relationship, a hobby, a habit, whatever it may be, Jesus says to turn away from it and follow Him. This is repentance.

This is not an easy believism but true salvation where one repents and turns to Christ by faith.

Mark 10:22 says that the man was sad because he had great possessions. He loved his wealth more than he did God. Even though he had kept the last six commandments, he had violated the first, and he was unwilling to let go of his god to embrace the One true God who alone is good.

Jesus is the only true and good One. All other gods but Jesus make terrible gods.

This man's religious tactic is still popular today. You and I have something in our lives that we know is not pleasing to God, so we double down on our efforts to do other good things in hopes that God will allow us our pet peeve sins. It does not work this way. God is opposed to such rationalization and compromise.

Note what Jesus did not do—He did not run after him or make an apology. No, He let him go. Jesus shared the truth and left the results up to God the Father. Jesus was obedient in sharing; the rest is up to the man—will he believe or reject? He chose to reject God and cling to his god of wealth.

In Mark 10:23, Jesus said it is hard, not impossible, for those who have riches to enter into the kingdom of God. Why is this? Most do not possess wealth but wealth possesses them; it becomes their security, their god. Homes, cars, large bank accounts create the false impression that one is okay and leads him or her to believe that they have no need for God.

This man was unlike Zacchaeus in Luke 19:1-10, a man who

was also wealthy but gave half his goods away and restored four-fold to those he had cheated. And remember what Jesus said, "Today salvation has come to this house, because he also is a son of Abraham; for the Son of Man has come to seek and to save that which was lost" (Luke 19:9-10).

In Mark 10:24, Jesus repeats what He said in verse 23, emphasizing it once again. Those who trust in riches are not trusting God. The rich young ruler would not turn from his wealth to Christ.

Jesus said in Matthew 6:24, "No one can serve two masters. For you will hate one and love the other; you will be devoted to one and despise the other. You cannot serve God and be enslaved to money" (New Living Translation).

Jesus next uses an illustration to support what He just said. This word picture in Mark 10:25 certainly illustrates well what Jesus has just said about those who trust in riches. Scholars I read believe that Jesus is literally talking about the small opening in a needle whereby you run the thread through to attach it. Threading the needle is an important part of sewing, but one cannot thread a camel. That is impossible, just as it is impossible for someone trusting in his or her riches to go to heaven.

The disciples were astonished at what Jesus said in verse 24, but in Mark 10:26, they were greatly astonished, beyond measure, extraordinarily—the Greek word is *perissos*.

They perhaps figured that the rich trust in wealth but everyone, rich and poor, trust in something besides God, so they asked, "Who then can be saved?"

Jesus looked at them, I think for emphasis sake; He wanted them to make sure they understood what He was about to say. Mark 10:27 is a wonderful promise, "With man it is impossible, but not with God, because all things are possible with God."

It is impossible for anyone on their own to be saved but not with God; He makes all things possible, even the salvation of the lost.

There is much we can learn from this encounter that Jesus had with the rich young ruler:

1. NOT EVERYONE WE WITNESS TO WILL BE SAVED.

Jesus Christ personally shared with this man and he turned his back and walked away because he loved pleasure and the things of this world more than God. So if people spurned Jesus and His witness, rest assured people will also spurn and reject us. If you and I can simply keep this truth in mind, then it will render powerless the two primary fears about witnessing—fear of failure and fear of rejection.

2. SPEAK THE TRUTH IN LOVE.

The Lord spoke the hard thing but also the right thing to this seeker. It was hard for this man to hear, but it was exactly what he needed to hear. When we witness to people or counsel with others, yes, even our friends and family, we must speak the truth in love, as Paul says in Ephesians 4:15, and as Jesus clearly demonstrates for us in this story. How many religious leaders will tell a wealthy man the hard truth and run the risk of offending him and having him go join someone else's church and give his tithes there?

Our responsibility is to speak the truth in love. Before Jesus gives him the hard word in Mark 10:21, the verse says He loved him. I am sure that love and compassion came through in what Jesus said and how He said it. We are not the arbiters of the message; it is not our job to make it palatable or easy for people. We have to share the hard facts that people are sinners, and the way they can be forgiven is God's only remedy and that is His Son Jesus Christ dying on the cross and rising again. It is not Jesus *and*, but Jesus *period*.

Truth can be hard to hear. But if we know the truth and do not share it because it is hard, then that says much about us. It is like a bridge that has been washed away by a turbulent flow of water from a breached dam. To wave people down, telling them they cannot keep going, takes speaking the truth because we have love and compassion for them. If they keep on driving to their peril, then your hands are clean of their blood because you tried to stop them.

A few years ago, I was teaching on evangelism to the college ministry at Central Baptist Church in College Station where Texas A&M is located. I was staying at a Hilton Garden Inn, and a fire broke out in the hotel. I had just come out of the gym and asked the person at the front desk, "Is this for real?" He said it is and I could see the smoke. I asked, "Should I go and tell people in the gym because they have no idea what is happening!" and he said, "Yes, please go." So I ran to the gym and warned those who were exercising. One couple was not too happy with me like I was ruining their morning, and I wanted to say, "Hey, all I am trying to do is keep you from dying!"

4. WITH GOD ALL THINGS ARE POSSIBLE.

"Looking at them, Jesus said, 'With man it is impossible, but not with God, because all things are possible with God.'"

—MARK 10:27

What a wonderful word for us—words of hope and strength. With God all things are possible, even the salvation of the rich. God can save anybody at any time.

Norm Miller is the former CEO of Interstate Batteries and current Chairman of the Board for the company. Regarding his testimony he says,

> "Well, I say that I came to Christ under duress. I realized that I had become an alcoholic and all of the life-trappings I acquired were no longer satisfying to me. I was an empty person. On top of that, I was anxious with the fear of failure.

> "It was around that time that a friend of mine told me I needed to read the Bible. It was God's Word and it was truth. I simply asked God to prove that His Word was true...

> "Then, I began to read the Bible to see what it said about me. I came across the Scripture in Galatians 5:22 where it talks about the fruit of the Spirit. All I read were the first three attributes and I realized that was exactly what I am looking for—love, joy and peace. I knew that if I had love, joy and peace then I really had life. Circumstances really didn't make any difference if I could have these things.

> "So, if this was the fruit of the Spirit, I wanted to know how I could get the Spirit. Then I read in Matthew 7:7 where it says, "seek and ye shall find." I told God, "I am a seeker and Your Word says that I shall—not may—find. . . .

> "From there, I went on to discover that Jesus Christ is the way, the truth and the life. I learned that I was a sinner separated from God because of my own behavior and faults. I knew I was a sinner even without reading it in the Bible. I knew it in my heart. It was in May of 1974 that I prayed and received Jesus Christ. I have never been the same since." [146]

Miller further states,

"Alcohol is not the only thing that can enslave a person. It enslaved me, but you may be the prisoner of something else. That something else may be gambling. I know guys who can't get through a week without laying down serious money somewhere. Their lives are out of control and they're miserable. But they're hooked. Or how about drugs? Or pornography? Or even food or tobacco?

"My point here is not to preach or lay a guilt trip on somebody. It's just that I believe a lot of people can point to some area of their lives where they're not free. They're caught up in a life-wrecking compulsion. Something else is in control. When I was drinking, for instance, I never meant to drink too much, but I always did. The stuff had me. I wasn't free." [147]

Think again on this statement of Jesus in Mark 10, and really let it sink into the deep recesses of your soul—"with God all things are possible."

Jeremiah 32:17 says,

"O Sovereign Lord! You made the heavens and earth by your strong hand and powerful arm. Nothing is too hard for you!"

All things—salvation of a lost loved one, a broken marriage, a rebellious teenager, lack of employment or finances—all things—God can make a way when there seems to be no way. He can work miracles!

We can learn so much from this encounter that Jesus had with a man known forever as the rich young ruler. He was a lost searching soul who came to the Source of salvation but rejected that salvation and condemned his own soul.

Whether you are rich or poor—surrender whatever you are holding onto and give it to Christ. Repent and believe on Christ, deny yourself, and take up your cross and follow Him.

Embracing Jesus by faith is not a leap in the dark but a step into the light. Take that step and place your faith in Jesus, turn from your sin, your little god, and embrace Jesus as your Savior and Lord.

Let all of us, as we pursue the ones God puts in our paths, learn from Christ's example and share with people. We must keep in mind that if they rejected Him, they will reject our message and us as well. We are not responsible for their response, but we are accountable to tell them.

CHAPTER 17

THE LEPER

When he came down from the mountain,
large crowds followed him.
Right away a man with leprosy
came up and knelt before him, saying,
"Lord, if you are willing, you can make me clean."
Reaching out his hand, Jesus touched him, saying,
"I am willing; be made clean."
Immediately his leprosy was cleansed.
Then Jesus told him, "See that you don't tell anyone,
but go, show yourself to the priest,
and offer the gift that Moses commanded,
as a testimony to them."

—MATTHEW 8:1-4

As a follower of Christ there is no excuse we can offer to lessen our responsibility when it comes to helping others. I find in my own life the primary prohibiting factor is selfishness. The key to being used of God more in people's lives is dying to self daily and saying to God, "Your will be done."

As we look at Jesus' encounter with the leper in Matthew 8, let's observe these four verses from the perspective of the Setting, the Sick, the Savior, and the Silence:

THE SETTING (MATTHEW 8:1)

What grabbed my attention was the setting of this miracle. Jesus had just preached the most famous sermon, the Sermon on the Mount, and Matthew 8:1 says great multitudes followed Him. Jesus spoke in a way the common person could understand. He preached with great authority and with enormous passion. Jesus lived the messages He preached, and the people trusted Him.

We need more preachers like this today, preachers who love and fear God, love people and will boldly and passionately proclaim the Word of God.

Notice that after this great sermon, a leper met Him. Jesus had the right perspective. He knew His mission in life was to seek and to save the lost (Luke 19:10) and to do whatever He saw the Father do (John 5:19).

If there are multitudes that have heard us preach, and someone very needy meets us, how willing are we to speak to them, stop what we are doing and minister to them?

Once as I was running at a high school track, I had gone around about four times and I was timing myself. As I rounded the track, I watched as these high school guys were hanging out and I thought about a sermon series I was preaching at the time. I asked myself, "What would Jesus do if He were jogging and He came upon these four teens?"

I had this struggle going on inside me because I was trying to run and train. I also have this song on my iPod called "Empty Me." I knew that if I kept running, I would hear this song and then be convicted further.

So I stopped, and breathing kind of hard, told the teenagers that I felt the Lord impress me to stop and tell them about Christ and invite them to my church. I shared the Gospel very briefly and invited them to our church. I had a good conversation with them and one of them invited me to their Fellowship of Christian Athlete meetings at school!

This happened years ago, but it also happened recently here in Austin while I was swimming and training. The Lord placed a person right next to me in the pool. I ended speaking with him and he even let me pray for him. I had to slow down and simply obey God because in my mind I was there to train, but God had a bigger purpose for me that day. In fact, I felt a distinct impression from the Lord to go to the pool that morning instead of my normal late afternoon/early evening time.

That is how I addressed the subject of spiritual matters to this man. I said, "I felt the Lord leading me to swim this morning for a reason and I believe you are that reason." I love his reply, "I very well may be!"

Jesus had just preached the greatest sermon ever to thousands of people and yet He had time for one lonely leper. At this time in Jesus' ministry He was very popular among the people. [148]

Luke's account (Luke 5:12-16) of this miracle relates how Jesus, after this miracle, withdrew from the pressing crowds into the wilderness and prayed: "Yet he often withdrew to deserted places and prayed" (Luke 5:16).

If we are to speak to men and minister to them, we must first speak to God and be ministered to by Him. If Jesus found it necessary to withdraw from the crowds and get alone with God for prayer and fellowship with the Father, then how much more must we do the same?

I read where one study revealed that the number one common factor among Christians who do not share their faith is they do not have a daily, consistent quiet time with the Lord.

Matthew 8:1 says, "When he (Jesus) came down from the mountain, large crowds followed him." The mountain was the place where He had preached The Sermon on the Mount. "The mountain" could mean the hill country located west of the Sea of Galilee. [149]

An excerpt from my Israel Journal reads,

"From the museum we went to the Mount of Beatitudes and this was one of the most spiritual times of the entire trip. We went to a church and read the Beatitudes from Matthew 5:1-17, and it was very moving. We then went into the garden shaded area and had some quiet time with the Lord overlooking the Sea and you could just envision how Jesus would have spoken to the multitudes of people who gathered to hear the greatest sermon ever preached. This was a special time and wish we had more time at this particular place."

THE SICKNESS (MATTHEW 8:2)

The crowds were following Jesus, and one of the first to greet Him, maybe the very first, was this leper. Leprosy was a dreaded disease during the New Testament period. The Jews hated this disease, not only for what it did to a person physically, but also because it rendered the person, and all with whom he came in contact, as ceremonially unclean.

L. S. Huizenga writes about leprosy and how it affects the skin, making it thick and scaly, especially around the eyes. It also causes the face to swell. The fingers and toes can be horribly affected, even falling off. The leper also emits an unpleasant smell or odor. Leprosy adversely affects the larynx or throat, causing its victim to speak in a very raspy, hoarse manner.

It is a pitiful sight. [150]

Leprosy had the connotation of a curse from God, as Miriam was cursed with leprosy when she complained against Moses in Numbers 12:10-11.

In 2 Kings 5:7, healing one of leprosy was comparable to raising the dead. [151] The lepers were shut out of the community, not because of contagion, but the fact that it typified sin and what sin does to a person—it separates one from God. The priests would freely touch the lepers, but the lepers were shunned and deemed untouchable because leprosy was associated with sin and the curse of God.

This man suffered the physical, emotional, and spiritual pain associated with this disease. Luke says in 5:12 that the man was full of leprosy, he fell on his face, and he implored (imperfect tense—kept on begging Him) Jesus, begged Him to make him clean.

In Matthew's rendering of the story, the leper came to Jesus; he did not wait or shout from a distance but simply came. Also, he worshipped Jesus and called Him Lord. The Greek word here is *proskuneo*; the common word for bowing down; it means to *worship*. Note that the word "cleanse" is used three times. This is the Greek word *katharizo*, from which we get the English word catharsis, meaning to *cleanse*. The second usage in Matthew 8:3 is in the imperative mood, *be cleansed*.

What faith and courage this took on the leper's part to approach Jesus, with all the crowds thronging around Him. He came to Christ, and I have found that when people are hurting and desperate and with nowhere else to go, they make their way to the Savior. The man heard Jesus teach and believed that He could heal him.

A few years ago, one of our mission teams from our church went to South Asia in ministry to our Unengaged, Unreached

People Groups. We went to a home where a woman had been demon possessed. She had reached out to Hindu priests and anyone really that might be able to help her. Finally, one of her friends said, "But I have heard about a Man named Jesus." This lady was desperate and allowed someone to pray over her in Jesus' name. Though she was at death's door, she was miraculously healed! She accepted Christ as Savior and Lord, and so did her husband and children. It was such a blessing to meet them and see them serving God in a tough place.

The leper knew Jesus was able, so he asked if Jesus was willing. The word translated "can" in verse 2 is the word *dunamai* from which we get dynamite. It is interesting to note that he worshipped Jesus and called Him Lord, *then* asked for the healing.

MacArthur said that to call Jesus "Lord" here is not just to call Him "sir," but is an acknowledgement of deity. He says,

"The leper came with confidence because he believed Jesus was compassionate, with reverence because he believed Jesus was God, with humility because he believed Jesus was sovereign, and with faith because he believed Jesus had the power to heal him."[152]

This man had saving faith, which leads me to conclude he embraced Jesus as Lord and Savior and he became, or already was, a believer or a disciple of Jesus. He had faith in Jesus to save him spiritually and faith in Jesus to heal him physically.

THE SAVIOR (MATTHEW 8:3)

In Matthew 8:3, Jesus reached out His hand and touched this man. "Amazing love, how can it be!" Jesus, the clean and sinless one, would touch a leper, and touch him He did! The man was immediately cleansed.

Picture in your mind the complete and quick reversal of all

we discussed earlier about this hideous disease of leprosy—his face, fingers, toes, skin, and throat—*everything* healed at the touch of the Master's hand!

When Jesus touched the leper, He would be considered ceremonially defiled and unclean Himself, according to Leviticus 13-14. Carson writes,

"But at Jesus' touch nothing remains defiled. Far from becoming unclean, Jesus makes the unclean clean. Both Jesus' word and touch are effective, possibly implying that authority is vested in His message as well as His person." [153]

I'm amazed at Jesus' touch, compassion, words, and healing. I love that part where Jesus says, "I am willing." **Jesus loves people**. He did then and He does today. He loves all people, the up and out as well as the down and out. It did not matter if His "one" was a leper or a Centurion, an adulteress or a Pharisee like Nicodemus—Jesus obediently ministered to those the Father placed in His path.

THE SILENCE (MATTHEW 8:4)

Jesus told this man not to tell anyone in Matthew 8:4. This is explained in Mark 1:45, "Yet he went out and began to proclaim it widely and to spread the news, with the result that Jesus could no longer enter a town openly. But he was out in deserted places, and they came to him from everywhere."

Jesus could not move about freely because the report got out about the leper's healing. **It is interesting to me that those Jesus told not to tell went and told and those He now commands to tell do not tell about Jesus!**

Jesus tells the man to go to the priest, make his offering, as a testimony (*marturion*), to them. The "them" was perhaps the priests or the people, but the significance of the act, according to Carson, and I agree with him, is that the whole scene would point to the fulfillment of the law and that is Jesus.[154] Yes, Jesus honors the law and tells the man to go and show himself to the priest and offer the gift that Moses commanded. But Jesus also fulfills the law, because He is the promised Messiah.

Carson writes, "Thus the supreme function of the 'gift' Moses commanded is not as a guilt offering (Leviticus 14:10-18) but as a witness to men concerning Jesus."[155] The significance of the leper going to the priest in Jerusalem and presenting his gift is further explained by MacArthur, "When the priest declared the man clean—as he would have to do because of the obvious healing—Jesus' miracle would be officially confirmed by the Jewish establishment."[156]

Lessons to learn from Jesus' encounter with the leper:

1. BEWARE OF POPULARITY PREVENTION.

Do not allow your popularity to prevent you from doing what God has called you to do and that is love and minister to people. Jesus was very popular at this time with the people but He stayed true to His task and loved people and touched the despised and sinful. He also made the time to get away from the crowds and get alone with the Father. Being in the spotlight and receiving the accolades of the crowds can be intoxicating. We must get alone with the Lord in prayer and get our priorities back in focus.

2. DO THE RIGHT THING.

Be real, transparent, and have integrity. Jesus did not look over His shoulder to see who was watching Him. He simply did the right thing and healed this man. If God ever allows you to have a significant influence for Him and you find yourself one day crowded with people who watch and admire you, and then someone, a less desirable person, approaches you—how will you respond to that person? Be real and remember that you are but a sinner saved by grace and do the right thing.

3. TOUCH THE UNTOUCHABLES AND LOVE THE UNLOVELY IN JESUS' NAME.

Jesus gives us such a stellar example for us to follow. Love the poor and unlovely like Francis of Assisi, touch the untouchables like Mother Teresa, and you will demonstrate your genuineness and be blessed by God. Your "one" this week could very well be someone that others despise or look down upon, but I encourage you to intentionally love him or her in Jesus' name.

FOR THE ONE

CHAPTER 18

NICODEMUS

For God loved the world in this way:
He gave his one and only Son,
so that everyone who believes in him
will not perish but have eternal life.

—JOHN 3:16

This is one of the more well-known and documented encounters that Jesus had with another individual in the New Testament. We will make observations about this encounter and hopefully learn how we too can be used of God to engage in dialogue those who are religious, intelligent, respected, but lost and without hope. Keep in mind that the most recognized verse in the entire Bible is given by Jesus within this evangelistic encounter or dialogue between Jesus and Nicodemus. Of course that verse is John 3:16.

JOHN 3:1-10

In this story we see Jesus directly confronting Nicodemus with the truth in John 3:3, that he had to be born again. At times we are to use a bolder, confrontational approach with people. This is the perfect approach for this man, because he needed such direct, intentional words to cause him to think correctly regarding Jesus and salvation. A friend in college used this approach on me, as I too was religious and lost.

Nicodemus is a Pharisee, a member of the 70-member Sanhedrin, the ruling, and religious, and political body in Jerusalem. Robert Coleman refers to him as "religious gentry."[157] In the New International Version study notes, he is referred to as a "blue-blooded intellectual."[158] Perhaps he is impressed by the Lord's righteous anger as He cleansed the temple of those who sought to profit off the worshippers.

Notice he comes to Jesus by night. Perhaps he did not wish for others to see him, as he is a respected religious leader and to be seen with Jesus would be looked down upon. Coleman states, "Yet he comes to Jesus. Why? To give Jesus some advice? To get information for the Sanhedrin? Or is it because he recognizes something missing in his own life? And why does he come after dark? To escape detection? To walk undisturbed? No other time to come? Or is he so anxious that he cannot wait until morning?"[159] But he comes nonetheless.

Here we have the Lord's encounter with Nicodemus the Pharisee and member of the Sanhedrin, a very prominent, influential man in Israel. The Lord met him at night. I assume there must have been some type of prearrangement for the meeting. What impresses me is not so much Nicodemus finding Jesus and meeting Him, but the fact that the Lord was willing to go and meet with him after what probably was a very busy day of ministry.

Dr. Roy Fish says here you have the intelligent, older, wealthy, theological professor coming to talk to the younger, less educated (formally), and peasant teacher.

Fish also gives the following characteristics of a Pharisee—

1. NARROW.

He had a thorough, strict, and narrow interpretation of the Law.

2. DOGMATIC.

The Pharisee interpreted the Scriptures in his tradition and was not open to another. However, Nicodemus was at least open, though a little, to what Jesus said and perhaps also by the way He conducted His life, as was evidenced by the supernatural.

3. A BELIEVER IN THE SUPERNATURAL.

Whereas the Sadducees, the other major component of the Sanhedrin and religious aristocracy of the day, did not believe in the supernatural, the Pharisees believed in heaven, resurrection of the dead, the afterlife, angels, and demons, etc.

4. A FORMALIST IN RELIGION.

He was concerned with formalism, legalism and liturgy, and more focused on the religion than in the relationship of knowing God personally.

5. A TEACHER AND RULER IN THE SYNAGOGUE.

The Talmud mentions a Nicodemus and that he was a very wealthy man and this could be the man in our text.

Nicodemus had a most powerful encounter with Jesus Christ. I believe he came to faith in Christ by what is recorded of him in John 19:38-40: "After this, Joseph of Arimathea, who was a disciple of Jesus—but secretly because of his fear of the Jews— asked Pilate that he might remove Jesus' body. Pilate gave him permission; so he came and took his body away. Nicodemus (who had previously come to him at night) also came, bringing a mixture of about seventy-five pounds of myrrh and aloes. They took Jesus's body and wrapped it in linen cloths with the fragrant spices, according to the burial custom of the Jews."

We also see Nicodemus mentioned again in John 7:50-52 where he defends the Lord. He sounds here like what we read about Gamaliel in Acts 5. The Sanhedrin savagely turned on one of their own in verse 52. And they insulted Nicodemus when they identified him with the undistinguished and despised Galileans. [160]

G. Campbell Morgan says the encounter Jesus had with Nicodemus was in three phases, or movements: [161]

1. Face-to-face in John 3:2-3

2. Mind-to-mind in John 3:4-8

3. Heart-to-heart in John 3:9-21

In John 3:2, Nicodemus gives Jesus a very high compliment and salutation by calling him a rabbi, a teacher come from God, and a miracle worker. He even acknowledged that God is with Him. These are lofty words of compliment and commendation.

But notice what Jesus did in verse 3—He confronted him very directly with the truth that he needed to be born again. Amazing. He, one of the key religious leaders of the day, needed to be born again, have a spiritual transformation of the soul. Dr. Fish says Jesus had to destroy the foundation of his faith so he could experience the change of life he so desperately needed.

The first small group I met with when I came as pastor to Great Hills Baptist Church was in 2010. One of the guys in our group met with his boss over lunch. He said his boss was religious in the sense that he would say he was a Christian, basically because he lived in the USA, and Americans are Christians. But over lunch he was lovingly direct with his boss and said, "I love you like a brother, but I would be remiss if I did not share with you how you can know God. You are my friend and I want you to spend eternity with me in heaven." He showed him the *Steps to Peace with God* tract and gave it to him. Great way to witness; it is both kind and confrontational.

I love the phrase "born again." I have actually read where those who follow Christ today are referred to as "born againers." The new birth is a spiritual birth where, just as a person is born in a moment in time physically, so a person is born again, or born spiritually by the Spirit of God, in a moment in time. **It is when the Holy Spirit comes in you and brings you spiritual life; it happens at the moment a person confesses his or her sins and asks Jesus Christ to be his or her Lord and Savior.**

When someone tells you they have always been a Christian, that is impossible. Because there was a time spiritually, just like physically, that they were unborn, and then they were saved. I think of Jesus' words here and try to interject them in the conversation when someone tells me that they have always been saved.

Now notice his response in John 3:4, a typical rabbinic response by following the statement with a question. He was confused. How could this new birth be experienced? A spiritual birth was incomprehensible to him; this whole concept of a spiritual rebirth was alien to this bright and influential man.

Jesus' response in verse 5 is to tell Nicodemus that he had to be born of water and the Spirit. There are a number of interpretations as to what this means:

1. Being born of water means you have to be baptized in order to be saved. This is called baptismal regeneration. But this is completely the opposite of what Scripture clearly teaches about salvation, that it is a gift of God that cannot be earned, as Ephesians 2:8-9 tell us.

2. Being born of water refers to natural birth. Jesus is telling Nicodemus that a person has to be twice born in order to go to heaven, born physically and then born spiritually. Verse 6 gives weight to this interpretation. Dr. Roy Fish says Jesus was challenging Nicodemus' belief that since he was born a Jew, a descendant of Abraham, then that was sufficient; he was okay and on his way to heaven. He writes, "Jesus then invalidates it all by saying that just being born a Jew does not get you into the kingdom. Physical birth is not enough...He needed the second birth because he was trusting in the first."

3. Water here refers to the power of the Word of God to cleanse. For example in John 15:3, Jesus said, "You are already clean because of the word which I have spoken to you."

4. To be born of water refers to the work of the Holy Spirit in the salvation process. Titus 3:5 states, "Not by works of righteousness which we have done, but according to His mercy He saved us, through the washing of regeneration and renewing of the Holy Spirit." This verse totally invalidates the first interpretation of baptismal regeneration. [162] Personally I see validity in all but the first interpretation.

Let us not miss the basic thrust of Jesus' teaching—everyone, yes everyone including the religious, must be born of God's Holy Spirit. A person is lost and in sin and he or she must ask Jesus for forgiveness and receive His Holy Spirit. And when this happens, when a person is born of the Spirit, he becomes a new creature, a new individual. There is a change in one's life because the Spirit of God brings about a change. If there is no change, there is no Christ.

All of us were dead in trespasses and sins, as Paul says in Ephesians 2:1. Until the Spirit comes in us when we repent and believe, we are lost and outside the security and salvation of

God. Jesus said in John 6:63, "The Spirit is the one who gives life. The flesh doesn't help at all. The words I have spoken to you are spirit and are life."

Jesus speaks a word of rebuke with firmness to the Pharisee in John 3:7. There are times in our personal conversations with people that we must speak the truth in love. When they are in ignorance and darkness, we need to speak the words of life by quoting the Word of God. We do not have to be arrogant or obnoxious but we do have to tell the truth.

In John 3:8 our Lord gives us teaching regarding the work of the Holy Spirit. Jesus illustrates for Nicodemus the work of the Spirit of God by using the wind to make His point. Nicodemus does not understand how a person can be born again by the Spirit. But it is still valid. He does not understand the nature of the wind either or where it will blow. He cannot even see the wind, but he knows it is there and it is powerful.

Merrill Tenney writes,

"The origin and destination of the wind are unknown to the one who feels it and acknowledges its reality. Just so, the new life of one born of the Spirit is unexplainable by ordinary reasoning; and its outcome is unpredictable, though its actuality is undeniable." [163]

In John 3:9, Nicodemus asked Jesus "How can these things be?" He is confused and has questions. Perhaps he is wondering how one is born again by the Spirit or how *he* can be born again by the Spirit. Notice Jesus responds to his question with a question; the Lord's question is to me a bit of a rebuke. John 3:10 says, "'Are you a teacher of Israel and don't know these things?' Jesus replied."

The Greek has the definite article (the) teacher. Nicodemus was an educated, learned man and he should have known about the teaching of the new birth from Ezekiel 36:26-27:

"I will give you a new heart and put a new spirit within you; I will remove your heart of stone and give you a heart of flesh. I will place my Spirit within you and cause you to follow my statutes and carefully observe my ordinances." [164]

Jesus continues His fair and firm approach with Nicodemus, a more direct, intentional approach than he used with others. There are times when we too need to use a more direct, confrontational, intentional approach so others can see the folly of their reasoning.

If you are interested in how to approach and dialogue with unbelievers in a reasoned, kind way, read Kelly Monroe's book, *Finding God at Harvard*. [165]

Be sensitive to those God brings in your path. You may need to respond with boldness like Jesus did with Nicodemus. Take some time and pray and ask God to help you see people as He sees them and then respond the way He wants you to respond.

In David Kinnaman's book, *Unchristian*, he presents the negative way young people in the USA view those of us in the church. The only way for us to change this negative perception is quit yelling at them from our steeples and get in the streets with them and tell them and show them the love of Jesus and His truth. I am so proud of our church as we make strides to do this very thing. We are becoming a "For the One" church that is reaching out!

I predict that there will be two types of churches in the future in our country—those that condemn at a distance and die, and secondly the churches that thrive by not compromising the truth, but lovingly sharing that truth as they get involved in people's lives and meet their needs.

JOHN 3:11-16

Let us look at these six verses from the following angles—instruction, illustration, and salvation:

INSTRUCTION (JOHN 3:11-13)

Jesus instructs Nicodemus the Pharisee in these verses. We do not read of him saying anything else—the dialogue now becomes a discourse of Christ. [166] He prefaces His words of instruction to the teacher of the Jews with these words, "Most assuredly." Jesus is saying, listen up, take special notice of what I am about to say.

Jesus uses the plural pronoun four times in John 3:11. There are a couple of ways to interpret the usage of the plural pronoun—one has it that Jesus is referring to Himself, His disciples and John the Baptist; [167] others see here a reference to Jesus and the Father. I believe He is referring to the Godhead, specifically to Him and the Father. Keep in mind that throughout John's Gospel you read of the closeness of the Father and Son and how the Son has come from heaven to accomplish the Father's will.

Jesus also uses the plural pronoun "you," which means He is referring to not only Nicodemus but also the other Jews. They did not receive Him. They had a record of rejecting the Lord's prophets and sacred Scripture. It is the same today as well. In fact, many Jews today are Jews in race and culture only and are basically atheists. I understand more the sternness of Jesus with Nicodemus in John 3:7, 10, and 12, from His words in John 3:11—Nicodemus did not believe; like so many, he did not believe.

It is interesting that Jesus uses the same Greek word twice in verse 11. The first usage is in the verb form we *martureo* (testify), and the second usage is the noun form *marturia* (witness). These words can be translated witness, testimony, evidence, report, or record. The English word martyr comes from this word. Jesus will die a martyr's death in fulfillment of John 3:16.

In John 3:12, Jesus makes another statement of rebuke and then asks another question. Nicodemus missed the analogy of the physical wind Jesus used referring to the Spirit's work. How then will he grasp the truth if spoken abstractly?[168] Others interpret "earthly things" as referring to the basics of the new birth. If Nicodemus could not grasp the concept of new birth, then how could he grasp "heavenly realities" such as Jesus' relationship to the Father, the kingdom of God, or God's eternal plan of redemption.[169]

Commenting on John 3:12, Pastor John Piper states,

"In effect He is saying, 'You keep pressing Me for deeper and higher explanations of the new birth. But a heart of unbelief, an unregenerate heart, can't ascend to the kinds of truth that I have to give you about the new birth."[170]

As I was studying this text and applying it to us as believers, I wondered how much more God would entrust to us and reveal to us if we would only believe what He has already shown us and take that to heart. If you are reading this and you have not trusted God in the basics of the new birth and you have never been saved, then you need not look for signs. Some have the mentality that seeing is believing; however, in truth, believing is seeing.

In John 3:13, Jesus makes another statement about His deity. He also has an indirect word for Nicodemus, telling him that in order to really understand this spiritual truth he had to look with the eyes of faith and be saved, even as those bitten by the serpents (Numbers 21:8-9) had to look with faith and be healed. He is further defining who He is for Nicodemus. No one except

Jesus had been in heaven and come down from heaven. There is much theology and instruction going on in this verse.

When reading the Gospel of John, it is so important to keep in mind the closeness of the Father/Son relationship between God the Father and God the Son. Here are a few verses that speak to that closeness and help us understand what Jesus was saying to Nicodemus in verse 13:

"For I have come down from heaven, not to do my own will, but the will of him who sent me."

—John 6:38

"Jesus said to them, 'If God were your Father, you would love me, because I came from God and I am here. For I didn't come on my own, but he sent me."

—John 8:42

"I came from the Father and have come into the world. Again, I am leaving the world and going to the Father."

—John 16:28

ILLUSTRATION (JOHN 3:14)

Jesus illustrates for Nicodemus further as to Who He is and what His purpose in coming to earth is in John 3:14. One commentary on this text reads, "Beginning in verse 14, Jesus appealed to an Old Testament illustration to make His point, further emphasizing that there was no excuse for Nicodemus, an expert in the Scriptures, to be ignorant of the way of salvation."[171]

Jesus refers to Numbers 21:4-9 when He says, "And as Moses lifted up the serpent." He is using this incident in the Old Testament, one that a scholar like Nicodemus knew and perhaps had even taught on, to point to Himself and the wonderful truth of salvation. Dr. Fish, referring to the Israelites in Numbers, says, "Those folks did not understand how, they just had to look. It wasn't necessary for them to know all the facts, just to look."

Jesus will be lifted up on a cross and die and all who look to Him and believe on Him will be healed of something far more potent than a serpent's venom; they will be healed forever of sin's plague and devastation.

SALVATION (JOHN 3:15-16)

In John 3:15, Jesus gives the key that unlocks the mystery of being born again—the key is faith or belief! The Israelites had to believe as they looked at the serpent on the pole, Nicodemus had to believe in Jesus as the Messiah to be saved, and you and I have to believe in Jesus that He died for our sins and arose from the dead in order for us to be saved. The key word is believe. Salvation never has and never will come through works; it comes through faith, trust, simply believing.

John 3:16 is amazing. John MacArthur writes,

"Verse 16 is undoubtedly the most familiar and beloved verse in all of Scripture. Yet its familiarity can cause the profound truth it contains to be overlooked." [172]

In the midst of an evangelistic encounter with a religious man, and in answer to his confusion, Jesus tells him first that "God so loved the world." God so loved, *agape*, this *cosmos*, this world of sinful people. Jesus did not say that He loved just the elect, but He loved the world. He created everyone and He loves everyone, even though all have sinned against Him.

Romans 5:8 states,

"But God proves his own love for us in that while we were still sinners, Christ died for us."

Some say you should not tell everyone that God loves them because God does not love everyone; in fact, He has created some for damnation. I cannot correlate that teaching with this clear word of Jesus in John 3:16.

I begin each evangelistic encounter with this statement, "God loves you." That is one of the reasons I like using the *Steps to Peace with God* tract written by evangelist Billy Graham.

The verse continues that He gave His only begotten Son, His one and only Son, the Lord Jesus Christ. Such a rich teaching here, please do not miss it. God the Father sent God the Son to die. "Gave" here is such an amazing word. God gave us His best, the eternal Son of His love. What He prevented Abraham from doing to Isaac on Mt. Moriah, He willingly did to His Son, Jesus—He allowed Him to die.

"Christ redeemed us from the curse of the law by becoming a curse for us, because it is written, 'Cursed is everyone who is hung on a tree.'"

—GALATIANS 3:13

"He made the one who did not know sin to be sin for us, so that in him we might become the righteousness of God."

—2 CORINTHIANS 5:21

I have a hard time getting away from that one word "gave." God gave. He did not withhold, but He gave and He gave His best, His very Son. We are most like our Heavenly Father when we give. Let us commit our lives afresh to be like God and give our best to Him. Give our families, our time, our talents, our resources—give our all to Him. Why? Because He gave and continues to give to us.

Jesus came from the Father in heaven to live among us and ultimately to die for our sins. He arose from the dead and ascended to the Father in heaven. And our response is we have to believe. "That whoever believes." Our salvation is not built upon our understanding everything or rationally figuring everything out; rather, we are to believe. Belief is the key that unlocks the door of God's forgiveness and favor to us.

Notice that, based on our choice, we either perish or have eternal life. We go to heaven or hell. Nicodemus cannot grasp it all but he can understand this! Even a child can understand this simple yet profound truth. Dr. Fish writes, "I can't explain it so you can understand it, but I can explain it so you can believe it."

Most have heard the name Charles Haddon Spurgeon. He was arguably the best preacher ever to live; only Jesus was better! He is in same category as George Whitefield, Billy Graham, and D. L. Moody. He served as the pastor of the Metropolitan Tabernacle in London, England, from 1861 to 1891. Thousands came every week to hear this Baptist pastor preach. When you study Spurgeon's preaching, you understand quickly the keys to his successful ministry—he preached the Bible, he made much of Jesus, and he, like Jesus, used stories and metaphors to communicate deep truths. He was a man of integrity who practiced what he preached and the people heard him gladly. His salvation experience is worth hearing if you have never heard it, or if you have, be blessed again by his story.

Spurgeon recorded in his autobiography what happened on January 5, 1850, when he was 15 years old:

"I sometimes think I might have been in darkness and despair until now had it not been for the goodness of God in sending a snowstorm, one Sunday morning, while I was going to a certain place of worship. When I could go no further, I turned down a side street, and came to a little Primitive Methodist chapel. In that chapel there may have been a dozen or fifteen people... The minister did not come that morning; he was snowed up, I suppose. At last, a very thin-looking man, a shoemaker, or tailor, or something of that sort, went up into the pulpit to preach... He was obliged to stick to his text, for the simple reason that he had little else to say. The text was "Look unto me, and be ye saved, all the ends of the earth" (Isaiah 45:22).

He did not even pronounce the words rightly, but that did not matter. There was, I thought, a glimpse of hope for me in that text. The preacher began thus: "My dear friends, this is a very simple text indeed. It says, 'Look.' Now lookin' don't take a deal of pain. It ain't liftin' your foot or your finger; it is just, 'Look.' Well, a man needn't go to college to learn to look. You may be the biggest fool, and yet you can look. A man needn't be worth a thousand a year to be able to look. Anyone can look; even a child can look.

"But then the text says, 'Look unto Me'...Many of ye are lookin' to yourselves, but it's no use lookin' there. Ye will never find any comfort in yourselves. Some look to God the Father. No, look to him by-and-by. Jesus Christ says, 'Look unto Me.' Some of ye say, 'We must wait for the Spirit's workin'.' You have no business with that just now. Look to Christ. The text says, 'Look unto Me.'"

Then the good man followed up his text in this way: "Look unto Me; I am sweatin' and great drops of blood. Look unto Me; I am hangin' on the cross. Look unto Me; I am dead and buried. Look unto Me; I rise again. Look unto Me; I ascend to heaven. Look unto Me; I am sittin' at the Father's right hand. O poor sinner, look unto Me! Look unto Me!"

When he had gone to about that length, and managed to spin out ten minutes or so he was at the end of his tether. Then he looked at me under the gallery, and I dare say, with so few present he knew me to be a stranger. Just fixing his eyes on me, as if he knew all my heart he said, "Young man, you look very miserable." Well, I did, but I had not been accustomed to have remarks made from the pulpit on my personal appearance before. However, it was a good blow, struck right home. He continued, "and you always will be miserable— miserable in life, and miserable in death—if you don't obey my text; but if you obey now, this moment, you will be saved."

Then lifting up his hands, he shouted, as only a primitive Methodist could do, "Young man, look to Jesus Christ. Look! Look! Look! You have nothing to do but to look and live." I saw at once the way of salvation. I know not what else he said—I did not take much notice of it—I was so possessed with that one thought. *Like as when the brazen serpent was lifted up, the people only looked and were healed*, so it was with me. I had been waiting to do fifty things, but when I heard that word, "Look!" What a charming word it seemed to me! Oh! I looked until I could have almost looked my eyes away.

There and then the cloud was gone, the darkness had rolled away, and that moment I saw the sun; and I could have risen that instant, and sung with the most enthusiastic of them, of the precious blood of Christ, and the simple faith which looks alone to him…And now I can say —

> *E'er since by faith I saw the stream*
> *Thy flowing wounds supply,*
> *Redeeming love has been my theme,*
> *And Shall be till I die."* [173]

Jesus is the Light of the world, and while believers come to the Light and are saved, unbelievers distance themselves from the light, become spiritually jaded and hardened, and condemn themselves to darkness.

THE LIGHT HAS COME (JOHN 3:17)

Jesus sets the record straight about God's love for humanity in John 3:17. People ask all the time, "How could a loving God send someone to a tormenting place like hell?"

The truth is He does not. When sinful man rejects God's offer of pardon and forgiveness, he or she sends themselves to hell. In verse 17 it is like someone throwing a life preserver to a person drowning in a swollen river. Is the rescuer to blame if the person throws the preserver away and drowns? No, the person who rejected the offer of salvation is to blame.

"When the time came to completion, God sent his Son, born of a woman, born under the law, to redeem those under the law, so that we might receive adoption as sons" (Galatians 4:4-5). These verses speak of God sending Jesus to earth to redeem. The Light of the world has come to bring salvation to fallen man. Out of God's heart of compassion He sent Jesus Christ His Son to be our Savior.

John 3:19 says the light has come into the world. The Light of Jesus Christ has come to bring hope and salvation, not condemnation. He loves everyone and the offer of divine pardon is extended to all who will believe.

"The Lord does not delay His promise, as some understand delay, but is patient with you, not wanting any to perish but all to come to repentance."

—2 PETER 3:9

Dr. Merrill Tenney writes,

"God's attitude is not that of suspicion or hatred but of love. He is not seeking an excuse to condemn men but is rather endeavoring to save them." [174]

God has certainly gone on record that He loves us and His desire is not to harm us but rescue us from the disease of sin. Max Lucado, pastor in San Antonio and wonderful Christian author, writes,

"There are many reasons God saves you: to bring glory to himself, to appease his justice, to demonstrate his sovereignty. But one of the sweetest reasons God saved you is because he is fond of you. He likes having you around. He thinks you are the best thing to come down the pike in quite a while… If God had a refrigerator, your picture would be on it. If he had a wallet, your photo would be in it. He sends you flowers every spring and a sunrise every morning. Whenever you want to talk, he'll listen. He can live anywhere in the universe, and he chose your heart. And the Christmas gift he sent you in Bethlehem? Face it, friend. He's crazy about you!" [175]

The Light has come in the person and presence of Jesus Christ, and there are ultimately two ways to respond—either we accept God's offer or we can reject His offer. Jesus explains both reactions as He speaks to Nicodemus.

SALVATION IS FOR BELIEVERS
(JOHN 3:18,21)

Jesus says,

"Anyone who believes in Him is not condemned, but anyone who does not believe is already condemned, because he has not believed in the name of the one and only Son of God."

—JOHN 3:18

"Therefore, there is now no condemnation for those in Christ Jesus"

—ROMANS 8:1

If we will pause and think on this glorious salvation that God has given to us in Christ, it will bless us to no end and put a smile on our face. We have peace and victory in this life and when we die we will go to heaven to be with Jesus. Jesus said in John 5:24, "Truly I tell you, anyone who hears my word and believes him who sent me has eternal life and will not come under judgment but has passed from death to life."

Notice in John 3:21 that Jesus describes a true follower as "he who does the truth." They are the same ones in verse 18 described as believers. Jesus said in Matthew 7:21, "Not everyone who says to Me, 'Lord, Lord' shall enter the kingdom of Heaven, but he who does the will of My Father in heaven." Those who genuinely believe will manifest that they are saved in the way they live.

Jesus also said in verse 21 that true believers will come to the light. We do not shy away from Jesus or refuse to fellowship with Him or His people. Rather, we love being in His presence and worshipping Him, whether it is in personal devotion or with the saints of God. We come to the light so our deeds may be clearly seen. We are not ashamed. We have nothing to hide.

Most of us are familiar with the wonderful promise in 1 John 1:9, "If we confess our sins, he is faithful and righteous to forgive us our sins and to cleanse us from all unrighteousness."

I John 1:7 is also wonderful. John writes, "If we walk in the light, as he himself is in the light, we have fellowship with one another, and the blood of Jesus his Son cleanses us from all sin."

The last part of John 3:21 reads, "so that his works may be shown to be accomplished by God." Our desire is for the glory of God. We walk in the light and we come to the light because we want our deeds to glorify not ourselves but the Lord. This verse reminds me of Matthew 5:16, "In the same way, let your light shine before others, so that they may see your good works and give glory to your father in heaven."

Those who really know the Lord have saving faith that is reflected in how they live and love. MacArthur puts it this way; "Saving faith goes beyond mere intellectual assent to the facts of the gospel and includes self-denying trust in and submission to the Lord Jesus Christ (Romans 10:9; cf. Luke 9:23-25)."[176]

The Light of God has come; those who respond in belief are saved. They demonstrate the genuineness of their salvation as they practice their faith and walk with the Lord. But for those who do not believe, their lifestyles reveal that and they will be condemned forever.

CONDEMNATION IS FOR UNBELIEVERS (JOHN 3:18-20)

Four times in John 3:18-20, Jesus uses a form of the word condemn. Jesus says in verse 19, "this is the condemnation." New International Version has verdict, the Greek word is *krisis*; other translations have decision, justice, or damnation.

Jesus is making a profound statement. And what is this profound word of judgment? Light has come but men loved darkness because their deeds were evil.

It is the same today. The Light, the Lord Jesus, the Messiah has come, but people do not respond to His light because they would rather remain in their sinfulness.

Do not miss the connection between what people believe and what they do. In John 3:18, Jesus points out the cause for condemnation—people do not believe in Jesus Christ. As a result of their lack of belief, their lives will be in line with their belief system. John 3:19 says their deeds are evil and verse 20 points out that they practice evil. The key word here is practice; it is a consistent behavior; it is who they are and what they do.

In Galatians 5:21 Paul also addresses the issue of habitually practicing sinful behavior, "those who practice such things will not inherit the kingdom of God."

The downward spiral in John 3:18-20 begins with unbelief (verse 18), then moves to a love of darkness and sin (verse 19), then goes to practicing evil (verses 19, 20), then a hatred of the light (verse 20), until they cut themselves off from the light (verse 20). The end result is condemnation; they are eternally separated from God because they have not believed and have refused Him and His offer of pardon and salvation.

One commentary reads, "Unbelievers are not ignorant, but willingly reject the truth."[177] Jesus goes on to explain further in verse 20. People will stay away from Jesus for fear that their evil deeds will be exposed. They become antagonistic toward Jesus and His church.

Newman captures the essence of lost people's rejection of Jesus when he writes:

"You Christians talk a lot about worshipping this god, loving Him, following him, serving him. Why?! Why do you think it's a good idea to follow a god who doesn't answer your most difficult question [the question of theodicy]? And, of all things, why do you let him call the shots about how you should behave, to what morals you should adhere, with whom you should sleep, for crying out loud?!' This is the real question behind some people's atheism, agnosticism, or skepticism.'"[178]

Unbelievers hate the light and they do not come to the light because their deeds will be exposed. This is so true. Conviction is a painful but necessary process. God convicts and draws you to Himself and everything within you fights against coming to God.

But when you do come to Him and confess your sins and repent, God forgives and removes the huge boulders of guilt and despair.

If we will only believe and reach out to God in faith, then the cycle of disbelief, condemnation, the love of darkness, the practice of evil deeds, and the refusal to come to the light is wonderfully broken.

Years ago, a young man quarreled with his father and left home. He continued to keep in touch with his mother, and wanted very badly to come home for Christmas, but he was afraid his father would not allow him. His mother wrote to him and urged him to come home, but he did not feel he could until he knew his father had forgiven him.

Finally, there was no time for any more letters. His mother wrote and said she would talk with the father, and if he had forgiven him, she would tie a white rag on the tree which grew right alongside the railroad tracks near their home, which he could see before the train reached the station. If there was no rag, it would be better if he went on.

The young man started home. As the train drew near his home, he was so nervous that he said to his friend who was traveling with him, "I can't bear to look. Sit in my place and look out the window. I'll tell you what the tree looks like and you tell me whether there is a rag on it or not."

His friend changed places with him and looked out the window. After a bit the friend said, "Oh yes, I see the tree."

The son asked, "Is there a white rag tied to it?"

For a moment the friend did not say anything. Then he turned, and in a very gentle voice said, "There is a white rag tied to every limb of that tree!"[179]

The discourse Jesus gives us in John 3 is, keep in mind, within the context of a witnessing encounter with a man named Nicodemus. Dr. Fish gives these concluding, practical applications of Jesus' interview with Nicodemus:

1. We should not be afraid to witness to the prominent or unpromising person.

2. For those who entertain false hopes, we must tactfully show that their present object of faith is inadequate.

3. We must keep in mind that a person will become a child of God only by spiritual rebirth.

4. Some people will be reached through the intellectual approach.

5. We must move from the general to the particular or specific.

6. One does not need to understand all of what happens to become a Christian.

7. The new birth means that there is hope even for the most sinful and depraved.

AFTERWORD

Our Lord obediently followed the Father's plan for His life. He has given us the model to emulate, and we too must love others and seek to introduce them to Christ. We are to follow the example of the good shepherd Jesus speaks about in Luke 15:4, who leaves the 99 to go search and find the one lost sheep and bring him home. We are very much like Jesus when we love the lost and get out of our comfort zones and minister to others.

For the Lord Jesus, His passion was pleasing the Father and ministering to others. I want that same passion in my life, to be so consumed with pleasing the Lord and serving others.

What if every follower of Jesus Christ followed His example and sought out their "one" each day? What if we began our day asking God to lead us to where He is already at work? Remember, God loves people more than anything, and it is His desire that all people come to faith in Jesus Christ so they can worship Him and live for Him forever.

Sharing Jesus with people every day takes a strong and vibrant walk with God. You have to daily deny yourself and fully lean into Jesus. But when you and I live with this "for the one" mentality, then we truly begin to experience the life God desires for us to live!

I have many men and women in the faith who are heroes and heroines to me. One of the people I have much respect for and whose example challenges me to share Jesus more is Dr. James Merritt. James is a personal friend and serves as the pastor of Cross Pointe Church in Duluth, GA. He is constantly pursuing his "ones," those God places in his path to share Jesus with.

I heard him share the following story of how God gave him the opportunity to witness to a man he had prayed for every Tuesday for years—Michael Jordan.

James was playing golf with one of his church members at a superb golf course in the Atlanta area. Two black Cadillac Escalades drove up and James' friend took off running to the parking lot because he knew who had just arrived. It was the greatest basketball player of all time—Jordan himself. "Pastor," his friend said, "You need to go get Jordan's autograph. He is right over there; go do it!" James declined and said he would just give Michael Jordan his privacy. Later on, while Jordan was sitting by himself in the golf cart, James' friend told him Jordan is there by himself and this was his chance to go get his autograph. When he said the words "this is your chance," James said he felt the Holy Spirit tell him this was indeed his chance not to get an autograph but to share Christ with Jordan.

Pastor James Merritt approached Michael Jordan and introduced himself as a pastor in the Atlanta area and then told him he had been praying for him for years every Tuesday morning. He gave him a Gospel tract and quoted Jesus' words in Mark 8:36 when He said, "For what shall it profit a man if he gains the whole world, and loses his own soul?" James said Michael Jordan had tears in his eyes and thanked James for sharing with him.

I pray this study of the life of Jesus and how He won men and women to Himself is an encouragement to you to go and do the same. God is for you! He desires to empower you with the Holy Spirit and use you to make much of Jesus to those you meet. Don't let anything stop you, no fear of failure or fear of rejection (which both by the way are rooted in pride). Love people and tell them the good news of how Jesus Christ saved you! There are numerous Gospel presentations you can share with those who need Jesus; some are on easily downloadable apps. I wrote a Gospel presentation a couple of years ago called the Five Crosses, and it is on our church app and web site at **http://www.ghbc.org/5-crosses**. It is very simple to use and is based on Bible verses you most likely have already memorized.

May God bless you and make His face shine upon you as you go forward in Jesus' name to share with your ones—today!

FOR THE ONE

NOTES

CHAPTER 1

1 B.B. McKinney, music; Anon. words.

2 Randy Newman, *Questioning Evangelism: Engaging People's Hearts the Way Jesus Did* (Grand Rapids: Kregel Publications, 2004), 14.

3 John MacArthur, *The MacArthur New Testament Commentary* (Chicago: Moody Publishers, 2015), 14.

CHAPTER 2

4 L. R. Scarborough, *How Jesus Won Men* (Nashville: Sunday School Board of the Southern Baptist Convention, 1926. Reprinted: Grand Rapids: Baker Book House, 1972), 18.

5 John Piper, *Don't Waste Your Life* (Wheaton: Crossway, 2003).

6 Brett McCracken, "The Perils of 'Wannabe Cool' Christianity," *Wall Street Journal*, 13 August 2010.

7 Rascal Flatts, "Changed," (Big Machine, 2012).

8 Jay Strack, Pat Williams, Jim Denney, *The Three Success Secrets of Shamgar* (Deerfield Beach: Health Communications, 2004).

9 Scarborough, 25-26.

10 Beth Moore. Twitter, 3 March 2018.

11 Scarborough, 24.

12 L. R. Scarborough, *With Christ After the Lost* (Nashville: Sunday School Board, Southern Baptist Convention, 1919), 47.

13 G. Campbell Morgan, *The Great Physician: The Method of Jesus with Individuals* (New York: Fleming H. Revell,1984), 15.

14 *William Tyndale: Opposition to Henry VIII's Annulment*, en.wikipedia.org.

15 Ibid.

16 Scarborough, *How Jesus Won Men*, 26.

CHAPTER 3

17 Walter W. Wessel, *The Expositor's Bible Commentary, Vol. 8*, Gen. ed. Frank E. Gaebelein (Grand Rapids: Zondervan, 1984), 632.

18 Controversial George Whitefield, https://www.christianity.com/church/church-history/timeline/1701-1800/controversial-george-whitefield-11630198.html

19 Wessel, *Expositor's*, Vol. 8, 632.

20 Morgan, 116-17.

21 Eduard Schweizer, from Wessel, *Expositor's*, 632.

22 Wessel, *Expositor's*, Vol. 8, 633.

23 Wessel, *Expositor's*, Vol. 8, 633.

24 Why Is Jesus Called Son of Man? https://www.desiringgod.org/interviews/why-is-jesus-called-son-of-man

25 Morgan, 119.

26 Wessel, *Expositor's*, Vol. 8, 633.

27 Wessel, *Expositor's*, Vol. 8, 634.

CHAPTER 4

28 Morgan, 18.

29 Morgan, 19.

30 Morgan, 20.

31 Merrill Chapin Tenney, *The Expositor's Bible Commentary, Vol. 9*, Gen. ed. Frank E. Gaebelein (Grand Rapids: Zondervan, 1984), 40.

32 Morgan, 22.

33 Morgan, 23.

34 Morgan, 24.

35 MacArthur, 115.

36 MacArthur, 116.

37 David Platt, Radical: *Taking Back Your Faith from the American Dream* (Multnomah, 2010), 64, 71-74.

CHAPTER 5

38 Morgan, 74.

39 G. L. Borchert, John 1–1, Vol. 25A (Nashville: Broadman & Holman Publishers, 1996), 201.

40 Tenney, *Expositor's*, Vol. 9, 54.

41 Tenney, *Expositor's*, Vol. 9, 54-55.

42 *Holy Bible—Baptist Study Edition, New King James Version* (Thomas Nelson Incorporated, 2001), 637.

43 *Holy Bible—Baptist Study Edition*, 1499.

44 Tenney, *Expositor's*, Vol. 9, 55.

45 Tenney, *Expositor's*, Vol. 9, 55.

46 E. A. Blum, *The Bible Knowledge Commentary: An Exposition of the Scriptures, Vol. 2*, Eds. J. F. Walvoord & R. B. Zuck (Wheaton, IL: Victor Books.1985), 286.

47 Blum, 286.

48 Tenney, *Expositor's*, Vol. 9, 55.

49 MacArthur, 148.

50 Tenney, *Expositor's*, Vol. 9, 55.

51 Tenney, *Expositor's*, Vol. 9, 55.

52 MacArthur, 148.

53 Tenney, *Expositor's*, Vol. 9, 56.

54 Tenney, *Expositor's*, Vol. 9, 56.

55 Blum, 286.

56 Borchet, 209.

57 Jim Denison, *Denison Forum*, Blog, 1 May 2018.

58 D. A. Carson, *The Gospel according to John* (Leicester, England; Grand Rapids, MI: Inter-Varsity Press, W.B. Eerdmans, 1991), 227.

59 Blum, 287.

60 Blum, 287.

61 Blum, 275.

CHAPTER 6

62 Morgan, 33-34.

63 Morgan, 35.

64 Walter L. Liefeld, *The Expositor's Bible Commentary, Vol. 8*, Gen. ed. Frank E. Gaebelein (Grand Rapids: Zondervan, 1984), 876.

65 D. A. Carson, *The Expositor's Bible Commentary, Vol. 8*, Gen. ed. Frank E. Gaebelein (Grand Rapids: Zondervan, 1984), 368.

66 Carson, *Expositor's*, Vol. 8, 373.

67 Tenney, *Expositor's*, Vol. 9, 201-202.

68 Morgan, 40.

69 Morgan, 40.

CHAPTER 7

70   Morgan, 29.

71   Morgan, 25.

72   Morgan, 28.

73   Morgan, 31.

74   David Herbert Donald, *Lincoln*, (Riverside, NJ: Simon & Schuster, 1996), 221.

CHAPTER 8

75   John Foxe, *Foxe's Book of Martyrs*, (England: John Day, 1563), 9-10.

76   Carson, *The Gospel according to John*, 158-159.

77   Carson, *The Gospel according to John*, 269.

78   Morgan, 42.

79   Carson, *The Gospel according to John*, 494.

CHAPTER 9

80   Foxe, 31.

81   Foxe, 32.

82   "The Fear, the Herd, the Witness," *Outreach*, (March/April 2008), 108.

83   Morgan, 52.

84   MacArthur, 71.

85   *Holy Bible—Baptist Study Edition*, 47.

86   Morgan, 50.

87   *Holy Bible—Baptist Study Edition*, 1495.

88   MacArthur, 73.

89   MacArthur, 74.

CHAPTER 10

90   Carson, *Expositor's*, Vol. 8, 223.

91   Foxe, 12.

92   Morgan, 107.

93   Morgan, 108.

94   Morgan, 109.

95   Morgan, 109.

96   Morgan, 107.

97   James Strong, *Strong's Exhaustive Concordance of the Bible* (McLean: MacDonald Publishing Co.), 9.

98 Carson, *Expositor's*, Vol. 8, 224.

99 Carson, *Expositor's*, Vol. 8, 225.

100 Carson, *Expositor's*, Vol. 8, 225.

101 *Reaching the Unchurched*, www.baptistmessage.com/reaching-the-unchurched-part-one, 23 May 2015.

CHAPTER 11

102 John W. Haley, *Alleged Discrepancies of the Bible*, (originally published 1875; updated: Whitaker House, 2004), 347.

103 Carson, *Expositor's*, Vol. 8, 200.

104 Haley, 347.

105 Carson, *Expositor's*, Vol. 8, 200.

106 Morgan, 130-131.

107 Morgan, 132.

108 Morgan, 132.

109 Carson, *Expositor's*, Vol. 8, 201.

110 Carson, *Expositor's*, Vol. 8, 201-202.

111 Carson, *Expositor's*, Vol. 8, 203.

112 Carson, *Expositor's*, Vol. 8, 203.

113 Kent Hughes, *Disciplines of a Godly Man*, (Crossway, 2006), 214.

CHAPTER 12

114 Morgan, 177.

115 L. Morris, *The Gospel According to Matthew*, (Grand Rapids, MI; Leicester, England: W.B. Eerdmans; Inter-Varsity Press, 1992), 401.

116 Wessel, 682.

117 Morgan, 178-179.

118 Carson, *The Gospel According to John*, 355.

119 Morris, 405.

120 Chris Voss, *Never Split the Difference: Negotiating As If Your Life Depended On It*, (HarperBusiness, 2016), 176.

121 Morgan, 181-183.

122 Morris, 405.

123 Carson, *The Gospel According to John*, 355.

124 Hughes, 96.

125 Hughes, 162.

CHAPTER 13

126 *The Believer's Study Bible*, (Nashville: Thomas Nelson Inc., 1991), 1508.

127 *The New King James Version*, (Nashville: Thomas Nelson, 1982), Deut. 22:23–24.

128 Carson, *The Gospel According to John*, 335.

129 Carson, *The Gospel According to John*, 334.

CHAPTER 14

130 Strong's, 50.

131 Walter L. Liefeld, *The Expositor's Bible Commentary, Vol. 8*, Gen. ed. Frank E. Gaebelein (Grand Rapids: Zondervan, 1984), 887.

132 Joel B. Green, *The New International Commentary of the New Testament, The Gospel of Luke*, (Grand Rapids: Wm B Eerdmans Publishing Co., 1997), 255.

133 Morgan, 121.

134 Strong's, 22.

135 Green, 255.

136 Green, 256.

137 Morgan, 126.

138 Green, 257.

139 Spirit of Giving, Gallupindependent.com. 12 December 2008.

CHAPTER 15

140 Carson, *The Gospel According to John*, 616-617.

CHAPTER 16

141 Morgan, 243-244.

142 Wessel, 715.

143 William Lane, *The New International Commentary of the New Testament, The Gospel of Mark*, (Grand Rapids: Wm B Eerdmans Publishing Co., 1997), 715.

144 Lane, 366.

145 Lane, 367.

146 http://christiannews.christianet.com/1097671515.htm.

147 https://www.interstatebatteries.com/about/leadership/norm-miller.

CHAPTER 17

148 Carson, *Expositor's*, Vol. 8, 128.

149 Carson, *Expositor's*, Vol. 8, 129.

150 MacArthur, 7.

151 Carson, *Expositor's*, Vol. 8, 198.

152 MacArthur, 9.

153 Carson, *Expositor's*, Vol. 8, 198.

154 Carson, *Expositor's*, Vol. 8, 199.

155 Carson, *Expositor's*, Vol. 8, 199.

156 MacArthur, 10.

CHAPTER 18

157 Robert E. Coleman, *The Master's Way of Personal Evangelism*, (Wheaton: Crossway, 1964), 29.

158 *NIV Study Bible* (Grand Rapids: Zondervan, 2011), 1320.

159 Coleman, 31.

160 MacArthur, 320.

161 Morgan, 67.

162 *The Holy Bible—Baptist Study Edition*, 1497.

163 Tenney, *Expositor's*, Vol. 9, 47.

164 Tenney, *Expositor's*, Vol. 9, 48.

165 Kelly Monroe Kullberg, ed. of *Finding God at Harvard: Spiritual Journeys of Thinking Christians* (Grand Rapids: Zondervan, 1997; IVP Books, revised edition, 2007).

166 MacArthur, 111.

167 MacArthur, 112.

168 Tenney, *Expositor's*, Vol. 9, 48.

169 MacArthur, 112.

170 The Son of Man Must Be Lifted Up, https://www.desiringgod.org/messages/the-son-of-man-must-be-lifted-up-like-the-serpent, 2009.

171 MacArthur, 113-114.

172 MacArthur, 115.

173 *C. H. Spurgeon Autobiography: The Early Years, Volume 1* (Banner of Truth, 1962), 87–88.

174 Tenney, *Expositor's*, Vol. 9, 50.

175 Max Lucado, *A Gentle Thunder, Hearing God Through the Storm* (W Pub Group, 1995).

176 MacArthur, 118.

177 MacArthur, 119.

178 Newman, 120.

179 Paul Decker, *Don't Be Late!* (Sermon, John 3:14-21, 23 April 2002), SermonCentral.com.

FOR
THE
ONE

SIGN UP FOR

DANNY'S DAILY DEVOTIONAL

Follow this link to Danny's webpage and fill out your contact information to receive a daily devotional via email. Signup is at bottom of homepage.

www.dfea.com

Or move your smartphone camera over this QR code to go directly to the page.